Are You Starring in Your Own Life?

1. You walk into a room, and:
   a) everyone gathers around you because you are so radiant.
   b) nothing happens. No one even notices.
   c) the room suddenly empties.

2. Your purpose in life is to:
   a) shine as brightly as you can, no matter where you are.
   b) ... well, you have a few ideas, but you haven't exactly settled on one.
   c) ... you are waiting to hear from your parents/boyfriend/husband/kids.

3. The last time you had a compliment was:
   a) five minutes ago.
   b) back in college. Or maybe it was junior high.
   c) ... you can't remember. Besides, who needs compliments?

4. The last time you gave a compliment to someone was:
   a) four minutes ago.
   b) back in elementary school. Maybe it was daycare.
   c) ... you can't remember. You have to *give* compliments too?

5. When you think about the costars in your life, a few of the things they have in common are:
   a) they encourage you, they have similar goals and they are unfailingly positive.
   b) they are negative, their goals are completely dissimilar and they always look on the dark side.
   c) costars? Who has costars? Your life is a one-woman show.

6. Fans of your body of work spot you and start gushing. You:
   a) stop and smile. You realize that their attention is a reflection of a lot of hard work.
   b) point out the flaws in the work they are praising. No one is perfect, least of all you.
   c) rush off to talk to some more important people. You just don't have time for it.

7. You've been invited to a fancy-schmancy event. In attendance will be the stars in your field. Problem is that you don't have a thing to wear. So, you:
   a) rent, borrow, beg and otherwise do everything you can so you can present yourself at your spectacular best.
   b) find something that looks OK. What do you expect at the last minute?
   c) decide not to go. Who needs the hassle of dressing up, anyway?

8. The last time you exercised was:
    a) this morning.
    b) when leg warmers were just coming into style.
    c) during your high school gym class.

9. There is a villain in your life that you believe is going out of her way to hurt you at work. Your response is to:
    a) look for ways of letting that villain help you. She'll either prompt you to look for another line of work, or she'll make you dig in your heels because all the interference makes you realize how much you love your job.
    b) think about that villain 24/7. So much so that her shadow is cast on virtually everything you do, including overeating, drinking, and taking drugs.
    c) spend every waking hour thinking about how you can exact revenge. Of course in the meantime your personal hopes and dreams get lost by the wayside.

10. You catch a glimpse of yourself in the mirror as you get out of the shower. You think:
    a) go, girl. Those spin/Pilates/kickboxing/step classes are really paying off.
    b) okay, so I really have the start that exercise program. Maybe next week or next month.
    c) gotta get rid of the mirror.

11. It's been a week from hell. You need to stop and relax. So you:
    a) go to the place in your home that you have set aside so you can take five. Here you can light a candle, read a word of inspiration, or do absolutely nothing at all.
    b) complain about how hard you are working to anyone who will listen.
    c) keep going at the same pace. You snooze, you lose.

12. You are facing the toughest crisis of your life. So you:
    a) cry. Get angry. Then begin the healing process, as you look to see how the experience can make you better, not bitter.
    b) pull the covers over your head. You'll deal with it later.
    c) get consoled by alcohol and drugs. They make you feel good, for the time being.

If most of your answers are A, then you are already Star material.
If most of your answers are B, then you may want to start polishing up some of your rays.
If most of your answers are C, darkness may well be overcoming the light.

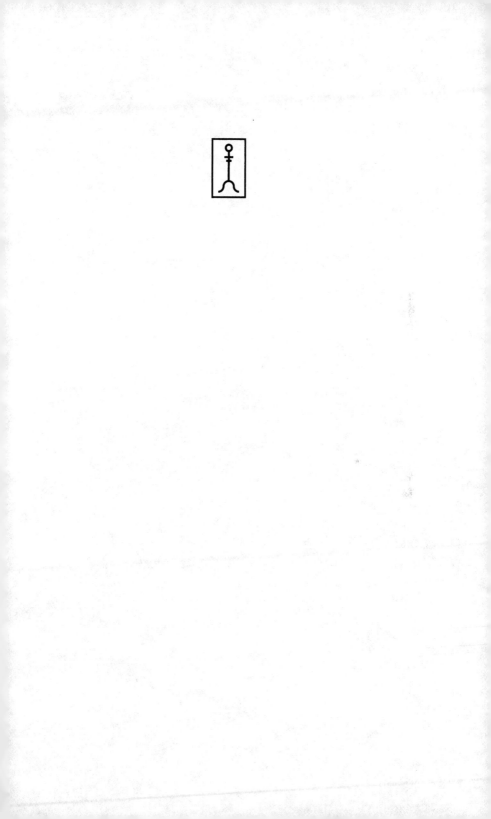

Reveal Your Hidden Star Quality
and Make Your Life a Blockbuster Hit!

Starring in Your Own Life

LENA NOZIZWE

A FIRESIDE BOOK

Published by Simon and Schuster

New York, London, Toronto, Sydney, Singapore

FIRESIDE
Rockefeller Center
1230 Avenue of the Americas
New York, NY 10020

For information about special discounts for bulk purchases,
please contact Simon & Schuster Special Sales: 1-800-456-6798
or business@simonandschuster.com

Designed by Bonni Leon-Berman

Manufactured in the United States of America

1 2 3 4 5 6 7 8 9 10

Library of Congress Cataloging-in-Publication Data
Nozizwe, Lena.
Starring in your own life : reveal your hidden star quality and
make your life a blockbuster hit / Lena Nozizwe.
p. cm.
1. Success—Psychological aspects. I. Title.
BF 637.S8 N69 2001
158—dc21   2001040072

ISBN 0-684-87308-7

For Mr. Leon Leaster Bothell, aka Malume.
You played so many roles in my life,
from surrogate father to steadfast fan.
I miss you so much. Whenever I need you,
I look up and see you shining down on me.
I look up a lot.

Contents

Twinkle, twinkle, little star,
how I wonder what you are.
— Ann Taylor

★

Introduction

The sunglasses were Versace. The outfit: Donna Karan. My attitude: exultant as I made my way from the first-class cabin to the exit gate at Los Angeles International Airport where the limousine driver was waiting.

The attention was not expected, but I have to admit that getting the Hollywood star treatment was great fun. Such sharp contrast to all the times I've landed at an airport and struggled to claim my luggage only to stand in long car rental lines. But to be honest the limo was not necessary. I probably could have floated to my hotel.

I had flown in from Washington, D.C., to meet with movie and television star Henry Winkler. The man I had grown up watching as "the Fonz" has added "successful producer" to his list of credits. He'd offered me a job as correspondent on a television show he was producing. My visit was arranged so I could meet with him and his staff.

The next morning Henry's partner and producer were the first to arrive to a breakfast meeting at my Sunset Boulevard hotel. Then came the Fonz himself. Even though the meeting was taking place in casual California, Henry was wearing a sports jacket and what looked to be a Hermes tie. The star of *Happy Days* had seen videotapes of my work on the Fox network, and he praised me for my ability to get people to open up. My ego was soaring. He could not have been more complimentary.

When we finished, I would leave for Paramount, where the show was produced. Henry was on his way to tape the *Larry Sanders Show*. But before we took off, our waiter stopped and asked, "May I have an autograph?" Henry graciously agreed. Then the unexpected occurred. The waiter turned and asked for mine!

There couldn't have been a better scenario. A glamorous location. A famous, generous costar and an ego-enhancing plotline that had me being recognized and courted for a job by someone I had always admired. It was a Sally Field moment. He liked me; he really, really liked me. I was glowing. In fact, I was shining like a Star. Who would have ever thought that a Hollywood scene like this would ever play out in my life?

Well, me.

It's the kind of scene I had been dreaming of and working for from the moment I aspired to Star in my own life—although I must admit that it would have taken a pretty inventive casting agent to place me in the role I have taken on for this lifetime. I had so many things going against me.

An Aspiring Star Is Born

For starters, my debut came about on a very humble stage. I was born in a tiny village in Malawi, East Africa. The most sophisticated birthing equipment in the small room where I came into the world was a wooden chair with a hole in the middle of it. That's where my mother sat as she awaited my arrival.

Even in utero, I had a flair for the dramatic. My entrance kept my mother and the midwife on the edges of their seats. You see, my umbilical cord was wrapped around my neck, not once but twice. What had once been my lifeline almost became my noose. Adding to the dramatic tension was the fact that I was silent for the first moments of my life. Not one wail until I was doused in very warm and then cold water. My birth was just one of the daunting odds I would overcome in a land where mothers have *as many as twenty* children because so many babies die.

My first big break came when I emigrated with my family from my beautiful homeland to America, the land of opportunity. We came out of Africa thanks to a network television program called *This Is Your Life*. Every week the program would feature someone of note, mainly from the world of show business. It highlighted the principal guest's life by surprising him or her with real-life costars and supporting players from that person's past. When my mother, Dr. Alice Princess Msumba Siwundhla, was chosen to be on the program it was the first time *This Is Your Life* had reached outside America for its star subject.

My *umame* (an African word for mother) had been born into privilege and nobility. Her father, grandfather, and great-grandfather (and so on) were African chiefs. After a blissful childhood growing up in Johannesburg, South Africa, tragedy struck. The happy young girl watched both her parents die from natural illnesses. To compound the heartache, villagers robbed *umame,* her sister Tillie, and brother Cameron of their inheritance. They even stole the blanket that covered the body of my grandfather. My mother could have given up at this crisis point, but she knew there was something more out there for her. At a time when women were discouraged from going to school, she was at the very top of the class. In fact, she was the top student of the entire nation. An impressive feat any way you look at it, but especially impressive for a woman, in those days, in those cultures.

My mother's academic achievements and the fact that she survived and thrived in spite of personal tragedy attracted the attention of missionary Josephine Cunnington Edwards. She in turn alerted *This Is Your Life* producer and host Ralph Edwards. As a result of my mother's star turn, I made my television debut in her arms. She effectively set the stage for me to follow my own aspirations.

Princesses and Prostitutes, Prime Ministers, and Pushers

Almost from birth I was an observer, and a quiet one at that. An introverted child who always had her nose in a book. I now realize that in silence I was starting to develop a rich plotline. I was weaving a demanding role that would ultimately take me around the world. A part that would allow me to traverse the worlds of princesses, presidents, prime ministers, prostitutes, pushers, and prisoners. But it was a role I would have to fight for, not unlike Hollywood stars who have to convince uncertain producers that they are perfect for a particular part.

To look at me, I was hardly star material. My looks and personality were a sharp contrast to my mother whose beauty was so legendary many of the girls and women from her village would ask her what her magic or *chitumwa* was. My two brothers were considered the good-looking ones in the family. In fact, "friends" of my mother would offer their sympathy, saying it was a shame my two siblings had inherited all the looks.

By thirteen, I was almost six feet tall and I struggled to gracefully grow into my new height. Other kids would taunt me for being too tall, too dark, or just plain ugly. Some of my older brother's friends would call me "Miss America 199-Never." Peers made fun of the way I looked and the way I dressed. My clothes were mostly homemade or hand-me-downs, unlike the stylish outfits worn by the "in" group. Of course it would make it all the sweeter, years later, when photographers from such publications as *The Washington Post, Newsweek,* and *Vanity Fair* would stop me on the street or at parties to ask permission to take my picture. It was sweeter still when strangers everywhere from the Midwest to Monte Carlo would ask if I was a star—a model, actress, or singer.

All of that would come much later though. As a child, the torment and ridicule were unrelenting. I now realize those experiences were just part of my character development. In the plot I was developing deep inside my mind, I knew that fantastic adventures would be ahead. All the pain I was experiencing would just make me a nobler heroine. That's what kept me going.

Sure, I cried. But all the name-calling prompted me to start digging deep to find the life I that wanted to live. So how far could a curious, tall, dark-skinned woman go? My conclusion after investigating the matter: just as far as she wanted.

Finding a Star Vehicle

I began concocting a rough draft of the life I wanted to live, what I now call my "life script." I researched my role in newspapers, magazines, television, and movies. *TV Guide* gave me as much direction as any career counselor. Black-and-white *Perry Mason* reruns inspired me to spend time at the San Diego city attorney's office. Though I must say, I never once saw a witness break down in the courtroom and admit guilt. The fuzziness of the justice system quickly caused my attention to wane.

CUT TO: *The Mary Tyler Moore Show.* The clothes were nice. Ditto the coworkers, although I kind of wished that Mary would stand up for herself a bit more. I wanted her to chase the big story on occasion, instead of spending so much time stammering, "Mr. Grant." Overall I liked her though. She was a professional woman in a glamorous career. She used her brain and maintained her femininity, so with the click of the remote control a career in broadcast journalism was born.

Journalism would become the perfect home for my insatiable curiosity; it would become my passport to exotic realms. The ideal setup for an action-adventure role that would lead to real chaos and scares and showdowns with villains around the world.

In a world where people judge you by your cover, I also began working diligently on my outward appearance. Reading beauty books. Studying people I admired. I became a self-Svengali, unlike blond bombshell starlets I have observed who never make a move without someone whispering stage directions into their ears.

Instead my aim was to pull my own strings and to take ownership of my stardom. Seeking a role no one could give me meant no one could it take away. By going for my role I could avoid "producers" telling me that I was too fat, too thin, too pretty, too ugly, too light, too dark, too young, or too old. I would take control. Like Shakespeare said, all the world's a stage. It did not matter if my biggest audience was in my classroom, church, or playground.

On the Air

It would take years and many rejections before getting my first job in television. Development of my life script meant going to school first. After taking classes at community college, I majored in journalism at San Diego State University. Thanks to a recommendation from a professor I got an internship at a KFMB radio station during my senior year. My work schedule was from four to nine in the morning. One semester I juggled those hours along with twenty units of class work. Needless to say I was not much of a party girl. In the same building as KFMB was a television station. Almost from the beginning I tried to worm myself into that side of the building. The weekend newscast director let me come in during his shift so I could do mock newscasts on the set, and one of the cameramen agreed to shoot stories featuring me doing on-camera stand-ups. In return all I had to do was carry his tripod.

I can't even remember how many people told me that I could never get on a television station in a city as big as San Diego without starting somewhere else first. I did not listen. After applying to stations around the country and getting multiple rejections I eventually reached my goal of getting a job in television news at my first choice, KFMB-TV. After a couple of years I even began winning awards, including an Emmy.

When I started wondering what to do next, critics told me that I could never go to a network after working in a city as small as San Diego. (Now San Diego was suddenly small.) Nevertheless Fox's *America's Most Wanted* and even people from ABC's *Good Morning America* came calling. My first choice was the morning show because I thought it would be the best stage for my abilities. Crime stories had always been my least favorite. Too often they made me cry. But after Fox made a firm offer, my agent went back to ABC executives and asked them what was up. They said they were still deciding. Instead of waiting for who knows how long, I made the decision to go to Bart Simpson's network.

By the late nineties I felt I needed to stretch my role again. I was seeking reinvention. I always thrilled to the challenge of writing my television scripts, so I began working on this very book. It was a challenge to write instead of sleep between television assignments. Some of the paragraphs you are reading were written in places as far-flung as Portland (Oregon) and Paris. But as determined as I was to have a book published not everyone was convinced that I should add to my role by writing. I would hear things like, "You'll never get it published," and "How can you go from being on television to writing a book?" One critic even asked me to my face, "Why are *you* writing a book about starring in your own life when you're not a big star?"

Expect similar doubts and questions when you reach for your star. It's those times when I take cues from the movie *Mahogany*. There is one scene when the title character, a model-wannabe-designer played by Diana Ross, is scheduled to appear at a charity fashion show. Mahogany plots to wear one of her own creations in the show instead of the fashions provided. Mockery and derision greet her as she vamps on the ramp, but she keeps walking, holding her head up high, throwing lots of attitude. There have been times when I have paused uncertainly on that runway of life, taunted by the occasional catcall as I pursued my dreams. But the trick has always been to just keep walking. And if you can muster the strength, *strut* down that runway.

Your Star Trek

Getting back to that question about me not being a big star. Many of us make the mistake of defining stardom by only the externals. Supermodel looks. Worldwide fame. Millions of dollars in the bank. But when the looks diminish, the wealth wanes, and the fame vanishes, the person who puts all her stock in all those things is left with nothing. If you want a visual aid for what I am saying just look at any E! *True Hollywood Story.*

The kind of stardom I am talking about takes cues from the enduring radiance of stars in the heavens as well as from the glamour of Hollywood stars. It's all about radiance. It's sparkle from within, when we know that everything is right from our motivation to our mittens. It's when everything works. It's a good hair day a hundred times over.

Living in the entertainment capital of the world, it's not unusual to see Sigourney Weaver heading to Starbucks during my morning commute or Tom Cruise going to dinner on my way home. After my close-up view of the very best the world has to offer, I have come to the conclusion that there is no one I would trade places with except the best version of me. Being a star is being the best version of you. It's a life spent polishing every ray.

I got to know many stars long before I ever set foot in Hollywood, stars like my home economics teachers, Mrs. Reynolds and Mrs. Roberson, who added glamour and grace to whipping eggs and basting hems years BMS (Before Martha Stewart). I also had daily exposure to the enduring radiance of my mother. She had written her own version of a family adventure role by leaving Africa, coming to America, earning her Ph.D., and lovingly raising three demanding children.

Your starring role is uniquely yours. Your parents or best friends don't select it. You do! Even though I am calling it a *role* of a lifetime, there is nothing artificial about it. When you take it on, it will fit you as perfectly as a couture gown. It won't fit your best friend any better than a role designed for Mae West would have fit Lena Horne or Audrey Hepburn.

Your Map to the Stars

Starring in Your Own Life will help you achieve and sustain your unique brand of radiance.

This book takes a multifaceted approach. Sparkling throughout you will find star points (★), which are easy-to-digest, bite-size tips along with five-star exercises designed to make you shine.

You can begin sprinkling stardust along your path immediately. Think of this book as a magician's bag of tricks. Reach into it every time you want to shine. If you want to get things jump-started turn to chapter 5 and learn how you can bring star quality to your every morning, starting today. If at any point you feel the compulsion to get your groove on, as I constantly do, let me direct you to the suggested soundtrack included in chapter 9. If you need to take a break at this very moment, go to chapter 10 where you'll find tips on taking five.

Having said that I should be clear that taking on a starring role is not just about instant gratification. The most fulfilling roles are the most demanding ones. There really is no such thing as overnight success. How many times have you watched a television show or movie for the second time, a few years down the road, and seen a newly familiar face—someone who is a big star now, playing a bit part then? I had to rub my eyes when I saw the movie *Coming to America* recently. There was an actor onscreen for only a few seconds, playing a robber, who looked very familiar. I didn't notice him years earlier the first time I saw the film. But it was none other than Samuel L. Jackson. The point is that it took years of toiling before he became *Shaft*.

Starring in Your Own Life offers guidance on making changes as fundamental to your life as going from bit player to featured star. Perhaps you feel that the role you are currently playing is too small, too constraining. Or maybe you are still in search of the role that makes you shine—your star vehicle.

Only you can make that leap to your starring role. I can't do it for you. What I can do throughout this book is be your fan and your coach. As your fan I will thrill to your doing your very best. That's one of the best parts of doing this. As your coach I want to share with you stage directions that work.

You've been waiting on the sidelines long enough. Raise the curtain today. It's time to write, direct, produce, and star in the role of your lifetime.

Shining star for you to see,
what your life can truly be.
— EARTH, WIND AND FIRE

★

CHAPTER ONE

Create the Role of a Lifetime

Begin Starring in Your Own Life

Get this. A really big star is coming for a visit. Think big. Oprah Winfrey–Leonardo DiCaprio–Will Smith–Tom Cruise–Julia Roberts–sized big. Elaborate preparation is common for cities and countries that spend hundreds of thousands and even millions of dollars to get ready for a visiting pope or president. How would you prepare for such a stellar visitor? Would you go on a crash diet to lose twenty pounds? Would you make a hasty visit to the beauty salon to give your hair some kind of style? Would you rush off to the mall to find a star-worthy outfit? Would you need a house-keeper to dig you out of your mess at home? Once your Holly-wood star arrived, what would you talk about? About what in your life brings you joy? Anything? What would you say about your job? What would you say about your personal life? Would you be tempted to embellish a little bit in order to impress this visitor?

But hold up. The person who I am talking about is not just coming for a visit. This star is going to be around for a while. In fact the person I'm talking about is someone in your city, someone in your neighborhood, someone on your street, someone in your house. You guessed it: the star is you!

By asking you these questions I wanted you to think about why is it we put our best foot forward for others. For many of us, our house is a mess during the normal scenes of our lives. But if company is coming, it's spic and span. And it's absolutely immaculate if we're moving to someplace new. When I called the repairman to fix a spot on my carpet, he assumed that I was moving. (I wasn't.) And a grocery clerk in Washington D. C. once told me that almost every time a customer buys oven cleaner, she finds out that the buyer is moving. It's as though we don't value ourselves enough to think that we deserve a sparkling oven. Or even more to the point, we don't believe that we deserve to live a sparkling life.

When you don't recognize the star quality within it means that you don't treat yourself as worthy of living your dreams. At the core of your starring role must be the unshakable belief that you are worthy. You deserve to live every day that same fantasy life you would want to share with your favorite star.

How can you expect anyone else to see you as a star when you don't value yourself? Wouldn't you think something was very wrong if you went to the shopping center and bought a 24-carat brooch for 24 cents? Not valuing yourself is equally strange.

"Role" Call

It's time to rise and shine. Stop disguising your true brilliance. You've been cheating yourself by going through the motions in unchallenging and unrewarding roles that don't even begin to display your full range. Or you squander your time and energy on pursuits that keep you from reaching for your star. You believe someone else is keeping you from your dream. You put down the dreams of others. You help others achieve their dreams. You live someone else's dream. You expect someone else to provide you with your dream. Or your dreams are stuck in the past.

See if any of the following roles sound familiar.

Damsel in Distress

Modern-day victims are so easy to recognize in film they've become a cliché. These mostly female characters don't have a clue when monstrous villains are looming. They make you want to yell at the movie or TV screen "Look out!" Once the inevitable chase begins, these Damsels in Distress often stumble, fall, or simply stop dead in their tracks. And they hardly do anything to fight back. One of the original movie victims, Pauline—as in *The Perils of Pauline*—was actually tied to railroad tracks as a speeding train approached. The Damsel is so popular with this culture that studies have shown that movie roles that "emphasize suffering and victimization" actually help female actors win Oscars.

Damsels in Distress always have excuses for not ascending to their starring role. It's always someone or something else's fault. The victim could have been the world's best student/singer/mother/salesperson/human or [fill in the blank]—if only her teacher/agent/husband/manager/masseuse or [fill in the blank] hadn't tied her to the tracks.

Of course at times we all feel like victims. I have catered enough pity parties to know how easy it is to slip into this role. Affairs where you could hear strains of the song "Poor, Poor Pitiful Me" in the background. But the Damsel in Distress doesn't just play victim one day out of the year. For her it's a lifelong profession.

Growing up, I saw evidence of the perpetual Damsels in Distress while babysitting. More than one of the mothers I worked for lived life with growing unhappiness. They felt great careers, great adventures, and great passions had passed them by. There were faint echoes of "If I hadn't gotten married . . . if I hadn't had any children . . . my life would have been so much better." But I could not see any attempt by these Damsels to do anything to improve the lives they had.

A major danger of acting out this role is that you spend so much time blaming others for the fate that has befallen you that you don't look for solutions. A favorite bit of dialogue for the Damsel in Distress is, "Why is this happening to me?" rather than "What can I do about it?" They hold to the belief that there is no way out just as tightly as Pauline is tied to the tracks.

Another drawback in playing a Damsel in Distress is that such a role tends to attract victimizers. I learned this lesson clearly when interviewing a young man in Brooklyn who had a history of being on the wrong side of the law. He told me that he and his criminal cohorts would go out on the streets and specifically look for "Herbs," people whose demeanor suggested that they would be prime victims. He told me their lack of confidence was always reflected in the way they carried themselves. Don't be a Herb.

I met someone who consciously chose not to conduct himself as a victim. When hosting a radio program about the AIDS virus, I began introducing my guest as an "AIDS victim," but he quickly corrected me, his clueless host, and described himself as an "AIDS *patient*." In spite of his devastating diagnosis he would not allow me to define him as a victim.

It's time to rescue yourself. Cut the ropes holding you back and get on the train. Today. Otherwise you will never know how far you can go.

★ ★ ★ ★ ★ ★ ★ ★ ★ ★ ★ ★ ★ ★ ★ ★

Make a list of everyone you blame for the difficulties you've had in your life. Underneath each name, draw a vertical line. In the left column, write out exactly what they have done to make your life impossible. For example: "My mother never loved me so I did not become all I could be." Or "My boss doesn't appreciate what a good worker I am and that's why I'm not going anywhere." Think of everything you can. Get it out of your system. In the right column, write out specifically what you can do about each item in the left column. Come up with all of the options you can think of to improve your situation. Options such as "Well, my mother has never loved me, but that is not going to keep me from the life I deserve." Or, if you have an unappreciative boss, start thinking, "If it's not possible to succeed where I am, I will search for a place where my brand of stardom is cherished."

★ ★ ★ ★ ★ ★ ★ ★ ★ ★ ★ ★ ★ ★ ★ ★

The Critic

You know the type. She doesn't think Naomi Campbell's legs are all that good, never mind her own gams are roughly three times the circumference of the supermodel's. She harps on the performances of network anchors, even though she fumbles when speaking out at the local PTA meeting. The Critic believes she can stir up a feast better than Emeril Lagasse and Martha Stewart combined. She just doesn't notice when friends surreptitiously dump her creations into planters. I recently saw a quote in a church bulletin that said it all: "A critic is a man who knows the way but can't drive the car." When are you going to get behind the wheel?

The Critic is a role that I have seen many aspiring broadcasters take on. There was one, whom I'll call Carmen Critic, who wanted to be the next Oprah-Whitney-Angela. When asked to research possible stories, she found that the assignments were never good enough. Yet she would not come up with her own ideas. She didn't want to make calls or check out newspaper articles. No, that was too mundane. What Carmen Critic wanted to do was go out into the field and fly to glamorous locations. When people with more experience were getting those assignments, she didn't quite understand why. And instead of focusing on learning more about the television business that she claimed held her interest, she spent all her time talking about the shortcomings of her assignments.

When you scratch the surface of these wannabe Roger Eberts who do a thumbs down to the world, you find that they are afraid of being unable to take on the roles of the very people they criticize. Dig deeper and you'll find that the reason Critics criticize is not because they feel superior. It's quite the opposite. Often the real reason behind criticism is jealousy and bitterness. These are caustic elements that can only dim your sparkle.

Critics are so busy giving negative reviews they lose valuable time they could be using to build up their own starring role. If you're a Critic, ask yourself: At the end of the day, what do you benefit from criticizing? How does it enrich your life?

I compare it to gardening. You can look across the street and see all kinds of things to criticize about your neighbor's garden. *Starring in Your Own Life* means using your time to make your own garden spectacular. Personally speaking, I always have lots of my own weeds to keep me plenty busy.

★ ★ ★ ★ ★ ★ ★ ★ ★ ★ ★ ★ ★ ★ ★ ★ ★

Every time you catch yourself criticizing someone else, force yourself to consider what would happen if you did the same thing. Then go out and do what you criticize others for. You didn't think Sally gave such a great party. Give one yourself and see what goes into it. You really think you could do a

better job than all the newscasters you see on television?
Then go on public access and see what it's really like under
the lights.

★ ★ ★ ★ ★ ★ ★ ★ ★ ★ ★ ★ ★ ★ ★ ★ ★

The Spectator

There was a young woman who, when she graduated from high
school, wanted to get into television journalism. Let's call her
Lena. She knew someone who knew something about where she
should get an education. This guy, we'll call him Sam, instructed
her on what school to go to and what classes to take. Sam was so
knowledgeable because he had dreamed about a broadcasting career himself.

So Lena went to school and graduated, as Sam the Spectator
watched. Lena went on to get her first job in radio, as Sam
watched. She was promoted to a job in television. And Sam . . .
well, you know. This Lena went on to win awards and even get a
job on national television, while Sam the Spectator never even
took one course in his area of interest. He was not sure that he
would ever be able to make it. So he did not try.

In Hollywood you will find a particular brand of spectator
called Hollywood moms, who watch on the sidelines as their children perform. Often those children are acting out the lives their
mothers always dreamed about. But spectator moms are not just
relegated to Hollywood. They live in a suburb near you, so ab-
sorbed with taking their kids to soccer, ballet, and karate lessons
that they find no time to follow their own star. Instead they live
through their children's achievements. They have either given up
on their own stardom or they believe it has to be postponed until
the kids get older.

Spectators are not unlike supporting players in the movies.
You've seen supporting players play the best friend of the star, but

they watch on the edge of the spotlight as the star lives out her dream. Spectators often glow when they are in the presence of someone who is living their starring role. The Spectator believes deep down inside that she's not as good as the star in the spotlight. She believes her rightful place is in the bleachers. That she is not good enough to be center stage in her own life. It's much more comfortable to sit at home and watch someone on television doing what you dream of than it is to do it yourself.

Let's call the next Spectator Katrina. She works in an industry where she is surrounded by some of the most beautiful and fashionable people in the world. But she admits that she doesn't take much interest in her own appearance. Katrina says she will not pay more attention to herself until she loses a few pounds. Of course, in looking at her, you'd never think she needed to lose weight. Even if she were heavy, I would advise her to turn on her television set to see a growing number of voluptuous women who don't let their measurements stand in the way of them looking spectacular. Instead I have actually heard Katrina describe herself as being "a friend of beautiful people."

There's another Spectator I know. Let's call him Boris. It's his personal life that keeps him from his true stardom. He is pursuing a career in music. Boris has won numerous awards and he even had a smash record in France. When I question him about increasing his time on stage, producing a CD, or making other advances in his career, he keeps telling me that he has to wait until he resolves his divorce. I've been hearing this for about a year now and I can't help but wonder how much further along he would be if it were not for his "I have to wait until . . ."

We could fill stadiums around the world with Spectators who have a bad case of the "untils." You don't want to take on your starring role—until. Until you lose weight. Until your children are grown. Until your skin clears up. Until you get more money. Until you move.

Unlike the Critic you applaud the efforts of others, and unlike the Damsel in Distress you blame no one for the fact that your rear is glued to your seat. But it's likely the reason you stay put is because you are afraid. Perhaps you're scared of doing well. And scared that it's lonely at the top. Well, it can be lonely at the bottom, too, especially if you are not fulfilled. What's been keeping you in your seat, rather than basking in the warmth of the spotlight? Is it stage fright? Do you think it's too difficult? No matter what your circumstances, you might be surprised by how much you can accomplish if you stand up from your seat.

In the movie *Ever After* Drew Barrymore spends a lot of time on the bench after she loses her father and gains a wicked stepmother. But then she makes the leap from Spectator to Star and even wins a prince along the way. Making your move can be equally rewarding.

★ ★ ★ ★ ★ ★ ★ ★ ★ ★ ★ ★ ★ ★ ★ ★ ★

Over the next week make a note of every time you see someone who is playing a role you desire. Any role. It could be a mime, a milkmaid, or a mayor. Once you've made your list, figure out how you can act out that desired role. Go perform on a street corner. Get a cow. Get the candidate application papers at city hall for the next election.

★ ★ ★ ★ ★ ★ ★ ★ ★ ★ ★ ★ ★ ★ ★ ★ ★

Ms. Cast

I once worked with a reporter who was extremely competent when it came to gathering facts and putting together a news report, but when it came time for a live shot this journalist, who I will call Ms. Cast, would freeze. She looked like a doe caught in the headlights. At one point, she was even taking antianxiety medication before her assignments. Live reporting is no passing phase. It's become the mainstay of newscasts I have seen around the world. It made me wonder why this reporter after so many years would continue to cast herself in a role that made her so uncomfortable.

I'll admit to have taken on TV jobs that I have not been suited for. And no matter how many exclusives I got, how much critical acclaim I received, or how much money I earned, I never felt good about what I was doing. One example of this was when I was considering doing a television program on a freelance basis. My romantic leading man at the time had seen a tape of the show and advised me to reject it based on the male anchor. He could sense from the tape that I would not enjoy working with this man. I took the part-time job anyway. It turns out this romantic leading man was very correct. I never had a good time and I never lived up to my potential in that environment. I always felt out of place because I turned myself into Ms. Cast.

When Doris Day was offered the role of Mrs. Robinson in the movie *The Graduate* she turned it down because she couldn't see herself "rolling around in the sheets with a young man I've seduced." Anne Bancroft would go on to win an Academy Award for that very same role. But Doris Day says she has no regrets about it because it was not a role for her.

You can avoid becoming Ms. Cast by doing a lot of research about the role you take on. I've come to ask potential employers, including Henry Winkler, what it is they like about my work. Winkler said my interviewing style, which I pride myself on. But had he said that he wanted me because of my physical resemblance to anchor Diane Sawyer I would have known immediately that I would be miscast if I took on the role.

When you're Ms. Cast it's like being forced to wear Laura Ashley when you feel best in black leather. Or it's being ordered into gray woolen stockings when you would rather slip on a pair of fishnets. We put on those gray woolen stockings for a variety of reasons. You take on a role to make money, to please your parents, or to gain status, not because it's a role that makes you shine. And even if the money and status come, as Ms. Cast you'll never feel quite right. The wrong role is an anchor that will always keep your soul from soaring. A sure sign that you have been Ms. Cast is that when you leave your misbegotten part, you'll feel perfectly content immediately—in spite of bills that need to be paid, glass ceilings that need to be shattered, and lonely Saturday nights spent with your pet chihuahua Fifi.

The truth is that when you take on your starring role, what you desire will come to you anyway as a by-product of your radiance. Don't limit your choices. You don't think you can shine as a caterer? That's how Martha Stewart started her homemaking empire after working as a stockbroker. Think you can't go anywhere teaching legs lifts and bun tighteners? What about Richard Simmons? (I can't think of another interview subject I've talked to who was more full of life and compliments than Richard.) It's a matter of how you do it rather than what you do. When you are cast in the right role you'll do so well you won't be able to stand it.

Sometimes we turn into Ms. Cast because we can't figure out what role would fit us better. Or we are afraid to make a run for what our heart desires. Coming up next we'll talk more about how to avoid backstage jitters and about finding the role that suits you. But I'd like you to start thinking now about how to make that transformation from Ms. Cast to Stella Star.

★ ★ ★ ★ ★ ★ ★ ★ ★ ★ ★ ★ ★ ★ ★

Make a list of all the times you have dazzled. It can be a memory from last week, last year, or the last millennium. On the opposite side of the list write down ways you can bring those warm, shiny feelings back through your work and play. Say you really glowed when you gave your high school commencement speech. Then determine how to incorporate more speaking opportunities into your life today by changing careers, or perhaps beginning to do engagements on weekends.

★ ★ ★ ★ ★ ★ ★ ★ ★ ★ ★ ★ ★ ★ ★

Latter-Day Lana Turner

Legend has it that Lana Turner was discovered at Schwab's Drug-store sipping a soda. (Although she said it really happened at a drugstore across from Hollywood High School, where the Sweater Girl was a student.) During a visit to the Cannes Film Festival, I saw dozens of starlets with similar dreams of being cho-sen from the pack. They drew attention to themselves by roaming topless at the beach for the paparazzi. I doubt if many of those photos appeared in any place of significance other than the private collections of the photographers. I certainly didn't see anyone be-coming famous—a Hollywood star—as a result of displaying flesh.

Maybe you're hoping to find a shortcut to stardom by getting discovered. But your starring role takes more than looking good, in or out of a sweater. Sure, things worked out well for Lana, but they don't always turn out that well. A starring role takes prepara-tion. Do your research. Study your craft. Be prepared. A starring role means paying your dues. Besides, if you're cast just because of the way you look in a sweater, your good fortune will last only as long as you are able to combat the forces of gravity.

Gravity notwithstanding, being a Latter-Day Lana Turner is no guarantee that you get the job. Journalist-screenwriter Aaron Latham recalls that during the making of the movie *Urban Cow-boy* the casting director presented him with two stacks of photos of actresses. One was comprised of actual performers. The other pile was made up of girls who were being personally "auditioned" by a certain movie studio executive. Latham recalls a young woman who showed up on the lot asking how to find the office of the aforementioned executive. "She explained that she was on her way to audition for *Urban Cowboy*." Problem was she showed up long after the movie had been cast. In fact it was on the very last day of shooting.

I have had a few opportunities to be "discovered" during my

career. One incident even happened in Cannes, although it was not at a topless beach. It was at the Cannes Palais du Festival during an international convention for television executives. I angled for an encounter with the innovative head of a TV empire. After stalking his exhibit, I finally tracked him down. I quickly gave him the 411 on my qualifications. His response was to name the hotel where he was staying. He went as far as giving me his room number. An insider at his organization later told me that at least one of his discoveries had made it on-air exactly that way. But sleeping with this television pioneer was not my idea of getting discovered for a starring role.

Latter-Day Lana Turners believe all they have to offer is their physical charms. But look deeper and you will find that you have a lot more going on than your more obvious talents. If you are counting on a Schwab moment, what happens if you are never discovered? My answer for that is: Discover yourself.

★ ★ ★ ★ ★ ★ ★ ★ ★ ★ ★ ★ ★ ★ ★ ★

Make a list of the proactive things you can do to "discover" yourself. Going back to school, taking refresher classes, considering a new vocation may be on your list. Don't wait for someone else to recognize your star quality. Find ways to put what you have on display.

★ ★ ★ ★ ★ ★ ★ ★ ★ ★ ★ ★ ★ ★ ★ ★

Neo-Norma Desmond

In the movie *Sunset Boulevard* Norma Desmond is ready for her close-up, but no one else seems to really care. Poor Norma did have a starring role, back in the day. But then she continued to hold onto the same dialogue and makeup in spite of the fact that the world had moved on without her. How many of us hold onto a wonderful past only because we just aren't ready to move forward?

On a plane trip back to California after a speaking engagement in Georgia I could not help but overhear a discussion about a Neo-Norma Desmond. A particular TV personality and former beauty queen had been invited to take part in a charity event. One of the organizers, who was seated behind me, talked throughout the flight about how this woman seemed to be mesmerized by the photos that were shown at this fundraiser from her younger days. The program organizer also talked derisively about how this woman stayed onstage much longer than scripted. By the end of the flight he had shared the story with at least half a dozen people, all of whom were laughing at her.

Perhaps you were the valedictorian in high school, or the homecoming queen in college, the wunderkind at your first job. But then you graduated or moved on to another job. Then what? When you leave behind the role of a Neo-Norma Desmond it is not just a matter of getting a makeover and a new wardrobe. It's about updating your dreams.

Neo-Norma Desmonds won't let go of the role that should have been long abandoned. Surely you know someone who wears the exact same makeup and hairdo she had in high school. Or maybe there is someone in your office who misses the days when there were manual typewriters instead of word processors.

There were lots of memories onstage at the Academy of Television Arts and Sciences when I went to the fiftieth anniversary celebration for a prominent Los Angeles television station. Former producers and on-camera performers were a part of the panel. The audience was rapt with attention as these broadcast veterans recounted their experiences. Among them was an actress who had gone on to some national renown. But the panel was suddenly sidelined when a former employee who had been sitting in the audience got up and commandeered the microphone. He reminisced at length, without regard for the panel that had been specifically invited for the event. Finally someone retrieved the mike from him, but it was clear that the man had stopped living after that job at the television station and appeared stuck in memories that were fifty years old.

Actress Ava Gardner had it right when she talked about viewing her old movies. She thought she was pretty back in the day but "much more interesting" in the present tense. "I don't hanker after lost youth or any of that rubbish. And I'll never be one of those women who look in mirrors and weep," she said. *You* need not be one of those women, either.

As I heard in a sermon recently, "a great past can never beat a great future." Can you recall any specific instance when you put all your energies into reminiscing about the past to the detriment of creating scenes for your future? Are you constantly talking about the "good old days"? In the last week, how many times have you wistfully thought about the past? Are the following words familiar? "We used to do it this way." "I used to be such and such." For your next draft, try "I am going to do it this new way."

★ ★ ★ ★ ★ ★ ★ ★ ★ ★ ★ ★ ★ ★ ★ ★

Make it a point to do something new today, even if it is as simple as trying a new route to work. Or try a new recipe, new lipstick, or a new aerobics class. Whatever. But begin setting the stage for a brilliant future.

★ ★ ★ ★ ★ ★ ★ ★ ★ ★ ★ ★ ★ ★ ★ ★

Breakout Role

Have you had enough of playing Neo-Norma, or Latter-Day Lana? Or the Critic or Spectator? Have you been Ms. Cast or a Damsel in Distress long enough? If you are fed up with your tired old lines and feel you've wasted valuable screen time, then tear up that old familiar script and gear up for the production of your breakout role.

My father told me the way to succeed
is to pick a star and follow it.
— BATMAN

★

CHAPTER TWO

Pre-production

Chart Your Course to the Stars

Star model Tyra Banks always pictured herself as a successful model. Even after one agency told her she was "too ethnic" and another confessed it already had a "black girl they were concentrating on," the determined beauty from Inglewood, California, pressed on until she was finally signed by the fifth agency she visited. But even it had misgivings. One of its representatives told Tyra that she had potential for runway work, but not photographic work. An agency "expert" told her bluntly, "I don't believe the camera likes your face." Tyra signed up anyway. She was going to prove that person wrong. These days millions of us have seen just how well the camera likes her face as well as the rest of her. She has been featured in dozens of magazines including the

Sports Illustrated swimsuit edition where she was the first African-American model to grace the cover.

There was a time in Jim Carrey's life when his income consisted of all zeros, not seven zeros. It is no accident that he gets $20 million movie paychecks these days. After bursts of success in early movies such as *Earth Girls Are Easy* and failure in his attempts to make a good living without working Las Vegas, he sat in his rundown Toyota on Mulholland Drive in Los Angeles and wrote himself a check "for acting services rendered, $10 million." The rest is Hollywood payday history.

Both the rubber-faced rags-to-riches performer and the curvaceous covergirl who refused to cower to critics had a clear idea of who they could be. They both had very specific visions of themselves for the future. Their goals may have seemed lofty at the time, but they had a target, and having a target is essential. If you don't have a dream, it can't come true. If you don't seek, you can't find.

Vision is the hallmark of successful producers. Before shooting a single frame, they have a strong sense of what the movie they are creating will be. Can you imagine how unproductive it would be to show up on a soundstage with a gaggle of actors and an expectant crew and not know where you were going? Improvisation will only take you so far whether you are planning a blockbuster film or a blockbuster life.

The Movie in Your Mind

When a producer I know, who has worked on projects with everyone from Bruce Willis to Drew Barrymore, goes in to sell a movie to a studio he can see the production playing in his mind. He has the concept of the film down pat. He sees the most important scenes. He hears the dialogue. That takes a good imagination. But even more important, that takes homework. Before making a pitch to the studio cheeses this producer has already begun the pre-production process. As the name implies pre-production is the work that comes before a shooting starts. During pre-production you begin the process of transforming an idea into actual production. In the process you clear up the details on the production design, or what your movie is going to look like. This is such a critical period it can affect the success of your production. I've been on television shoots myself where producers were not clear before shooting about what they needed in terms of interviews and video. In the end those producers would try to patch together something in the edit room. The results were far from stellar.

Of course visualization pays off in real life as well. Everything that I have really wanted, I got—everything—after I first conjured up my goals as a movie in my mind. In college, I took classes by day and folded sweaters by night. But in my mind I was a television correspondent. I saw myself heading to work. I imagined what it would be like to go out on a story. I even dreamed of getting awards. I kept replaying those scenes until I actually lived them out.

When I was going through the process of getting this book published I could see it on bookstore shelves in my mind's movie. Before a publisher accepted it, I could see in my mind's eye readers curled up on couches getting something out of it. Mind you these were not blurry dream sequences. The scenes were as clear and tangible as any cinema verité production. I don't believe the real scenes of selling the book or becoming a television correspondent would have ever happened without the previews. Similarly Jim and Tyra achieved their goals because they were substantive, not gossamer dreams on wings.

Become a Figment of Your Imagination

When you close your eyes are images of your fantasy life emerging? Or are you drawing a blank? Maybe all you can see is just a series of vague images that don't go anywhere. Let's work together to fill in the blanks. Be thoughtful and honest about what it is that you want. Be open to every possibility. Don't reject an idea just because you think you're too old or too heavy or too poor or too anything to achieve it.

Follow your interests and as author Joseph Campbell says, "Follow your bliss." Over and over again I hear successful filmmakers say they choose only projects that excite them. When you think of your role I want you to tingle, glow, and feel alive. Make it something that you love with all of your heart. Hold absolutely nothing back. Don't settle. And the more clearly you can see this vision the better your chances will be that you will achieve it.

As you concoct this starring vehicle, think BIG. Star talk show host Oprah Winfrey says too many women have small dreams, especially if they have been abused. So the dream is to become a paralegal, instead of a lawyer. A medical assistant instead of a doctor. The aide-de-camp instead of the manager of a homeless shelter. Eleanor Roosevelt said, "You must do the things that you think you can not do." If you need a reminder of how big your role can be, refer to the cover of this book. Remember it says *starring* in your own life, not bit playing.

So prod your imagination and reflect on the happiest moments in your life so far. Dig up old photo albums. Look for the pictures of you beaming the brightest. Are you shining when you are on the softball field? The day you got your first job? The day you got married? How can you bring that quality to your life today? Ideas could include taking up a sport, getting a job outside of your home, rekindling the feelings you had on the day of betrothal. Review home videos and take notes of what you focus on when you are on holiday. Are vacation videos filled with close-ups of architecture? Street fashion? Children?

If you don't have it on tape or video, mentally rewind childhood memories. Search for your happiest moments. *Diagnosis Murder* executive producer Chris Abbott tells me she would write, produce, and then act in shows she presented to fellow kindergartners. These activities foreshadowed her adult life. First there was acting in musicals and television commercials. Chris, who was selected as one of *Variety* magazine's "50 to Watch," then started writing and producing. Her credits include *Little House on the Prairie; B.L. Stryker; Dr. Quinn, Medicine Woman; Cagney and Lacey;* and *Magnum P.I.*

Research and Development

Revisiting memory lane is just the beginning of your pre-production research. The other essential element here is doing your homework. There was a time when a certain movie producer could not afford to buy industry dailies. So he would go to the newsstands and read as much as he could off the front page. That determination to get information is one of the reasons he went on to produce multimillion-dollar productions.

In order to let your imagination go wild, you need to consider all of the possibilities, which means trips to the library, the information superhighway, and, yes, the newsstand. Sometimes, we only have a foggy notion of what we want to focus on. Say you kind of have an idea of doing something that involves teaching. On what level? Elementary or high school? Where? What kind of institution? Public or private? That's where research is key. Only through research can you make educated choices about developing your life into what you want it to be. Research will especially help if you have absolutely no idea of what you are looking for. In that case simply pick up every single book, magazine, and newspaper that's even of the vaguest interest, to see if your dreams are hidden within the pages. This is not a drudgery-filled school assignment. Remember finding your star is fun. Be open to anything and everything that captures your heart. Let your mind skip, run, and play.

Bring home any books that inspire you. Don't neglect international magazines and newspapers. Be global as you search for people who are now living out aspects of your dream life. Look to see what their first steps were in achieving the goals.

★ If you can find an address, drop your role model a note with questions that you are dying to know the answers to.

★ Do your research up-close and personal. Join an organization that is made up of the kind of people you want to be like and observe details from their lives. Take notes on everything from their families to their faith, from their cars to their charisma, from their wardrobes to their woes. Who makes up their circle of supporting players, costars, and fans? What motivates them? Where do they shop? How do they live? Observe. Ask. If you find that you consistently don't like what you see, reexamine what it is that you want to do with your life.

★ When you are in a crowd who captures your interest? When I was still in school in San Diego I began making trips to Los Angeles. My most exciting sightings were not of Hollywood stars, but of the behind-the-scenes powers such as Suzanne de Passe, Aaron Spelling, Lew Wasserman, or Grant Tinker. So I guess it's not surprising that I grew up wanting to produce my own television projects even if it turned out they were for the evening news. When I spent a lot of time on the East Coast my television agent would host lavish dinner parties at his New York apartment. He would invite a collection of television journalists along with writers whose work appeared in publications such as *Harper's Bazaar, New York* magazine, and *The New York Times*. My attention always focused on the writers. Keep track of who gets your attention.

★ Figure out how you can go on location to your fantasy world. After learning that some well-known TV personalities got their first jobs after visiting friends in newsrooms, I made sure to visit anyone I knew who worked in one. As it happened, more than one executive wanted to know more about me because of those appearances.

★ Don't be afraid to look outside the norm for your role. Emmy Award–winning actress Camryn Manheim became very frustrated in her search for her place in Hollywood. Tired of being cast as the butt-of-all-jokes fat girl, she asked her agent to start putting her up for male parts. As a result, she got offered a wider range of roles, some of which were originally written for guys. Ignore those who think you should be typecast and go for roles even if they are outside of the norm for your weight, sex, race, or bust size.

★ Pay attention to how you dress for Halloween. Why not stretch out the role that makes you beam for more than one day out of the year?

Picking Your Genre

It would be almost impossible for a producer to talk about her movie project without saying what the *genre* is. Figuring out which category a production falls into can provide clues on everything from the set and wardrobe to the budget and cast. The research that you've done so far will be a guide to which genre or genres to choose. Selecting the genre for your life can also be especially helpful if you are having difficulty picturing your life script. As I said earlier, your life script is what I call the plot that you have for your life—your month, five-week, or five-year plan.

Your choice must be consistent with your desires and dreams. For example, a really great sense of humor is essential if you decide comedy is your genre. If you pick family, children will likely play a role in your life script. If you go Western, you may want to check out how good you look in chaps.

A Sampling of Genres

Action, adventure, ancient world, animal, buddy, caper, comedy, coming-of-age, crime, drama, family, fantasy, historical, horror, musical, mystery, parody, political, romance, science fiction, suspense, thriller, war, Western

★

I've always been drawn to intrigue, travel, and excitement, so it made complete sense that I would choose the action-adventure genre for my life. So it's no wonder that when I watched *Mission: Impossible 2,* I pictured myself in Tom Cruise's role, rather than the one of his romantic lead played by the African-born Thandie Newton. Yes, she is stunningly beautiful, but what I wanted was to race around in cars and motorcycles.

As a consequence of me recognizing that I wanted to live life as a cliffhanger, I was on my hands and knees looking for clues in the bedroom of spree-killer Andrew Cunanan. He was still on the run at the time and could have returned to his apartment at any time. There was more action and adventure when I was forced into hiding after asking a notorious subject with a killer reputation a few questions he wasn't too fond of.

There have also been visits to prisons and bordellos around the

world. I've spent more time with runaways, taggers, and prosti
tutes than anyone I know.

Virtually every aspect of my life I view through the prism of my
genre. The setbacks and disappointments mark the beginning of
new adventures. And my action-adventure does not always take
place in exotic locations. It can also unfold at the grocery store,
during a session in the kitchen, or playing in a room filled with
children. Even spending time in a solitary room with my computer writing this book has been an adventure. Between pound-
ing out pages I think of all the places the words I am writing will
take me. Your genre grows and adapts with you.

My literary agent, Jenny Bent, not only likes to watch romantic
comedies, she likes to live them. Her choice of genre fits her married life, which is filled with fun and laughter. Hollywood agent
Pat Quinn, a former Warner Bros. executive and Sundance Film
Institute fund-raiser, tells me her ideal life is a Noel Coward production. The knighted author and playwright who wrote *Private
Lies, Design for Living,* and *Blithe Spirit* was known for his sophisticated yet naïve heroines. The optimistic nature of musical comedies makes them the perfect combo for author and script
consultant Dr. Linda Seger. She tells me her favorite of all is *The
Sound of Music.* She thinks the best line is: "God never closes a
door without opening a window," words that are a reflection of
her background that includes advanced degrees in both theology
and drama.

Now it's your time to choose. What genre best describes your
dream role? Select as many as appropriate. Don't be timid about
mixing it up. Why not a comedy-family-sci-fi-western?

 If it's taking a while to zero in on your genre, go through old
video rental receipts to see if there is a type of movie that you
just keep renting over and over again.

 Also note where you gravitate when you go to the library or
magazine rack. Note the arrays of genres featured there.

Interest in magazines on parenting would suggest your genre is family. If you go for *Travel + Leisure,* perhaps you, too, want an action-adventure life. If you pick up *Analog* magazine, then sci-fi.

Setting

What is the location you think of when you conjure up images of the movie in your mind? A tropical island? A high-rise office building? Or a classroom filled with the laughter of children? Location managers spend days looking for the perfect spot to shoot a particular scene. What kind of thought have you given to scouting the *setting* for your starring role?

Location, location, location is not just important to real estate brokers. It's an important factor as you create your starring role. Let's say you have decided to become the world's next supermodel but you are living in the Midwest in a place with a population of twenty-five. You will probably have better luck moving to a model mecca such as Milan, New York, Los Angeles, Paris, or South Beach. Perhaps you long for a bucolic setting, say, on a farm that stretches for acres? Not a likely possibility if your zip code is 90210.

Or maybe you would prefer to have multiple settings as I did for several bicoastal years when I split my time between Washington, D.C., and San Diego. I got the coast and I got the culture, shuttling between world-class museums and world-class beaches. My multiple locations were a perfect match for my action-adventure genre.

★ Again check back to those movie rental receipts. What settings excite you? Perhaps you go for the exotic locations featured in such films as *The Beach, The Year of Living Dangerously,* or *Out of Africa.* Or maybe you are more impressed by the urban settings of *The Bonfire of the Vanities,*

Jungle Fever, or *Do the Right Thing.* Then again the pastoral setting of *Coal Miner's Daughter* might do it for you.

★ Does a certain kind of workplace seem to keep showing up in the films and television programs you favor? Are you transfixed by *Mary Tyler Moore Show* reruns? Have you rented the movies *Broadcast News* and *Up Close and Personal* repeatedly? Then maybe you really do want a job in television news.

★ Once you have figured out your ultimate setting, use paints, construction paper—whatever it takes to create dream sets. Then let your imagination wander through them.

Budget

It cost somewhere around $200 million to bring the movie *Titanic* to the big screen. The price for *The Blair Witch Project* was in the much less tony neighborhood of $300,000. But one thing both movies have in common is that they are certifiable blockbusters. Your *budget,* big or small, is no excuse for you not to create your own hit. We often blame our bank accounts for the lack of sparkle. Christina Onassis was known to blame her unhappy life on the fact that she had too much money. But I am sure that you know someone (maybe it's you) who points to insufficient funds as the reason for not shining. If you're worrying that you can't afford to bring your starring role to life, the truth is you cannot afford *not* to. When it comes to budget, size does not matter. Determination does.

Now it's true that in Hollywood a budget can sometimes mean the difference between casting an A or C list actor. But then how many times have you seen a big Hollywood star doing a movie just because the project was worthy? Bottom line: You will be surprised to see how much you can accomplish with a small budget when you have a deserving project. You can enlist a lot of support with a worthy endeavor.

Money itself cannot automatically take away or give you glow. I know that during times of prosperity, I have not always spent my money on people, places, and things that have added to my star shine. And then there is my mother. There was absolutely no money for her to fund the fantastic dream of this orphan girl from Africa. Even when avaricious villagers stole everything she was able to parlay the currency of faith and resolve into a fantastic voyage to America. Still on a tiny budget she went on to achieve her goal of earning a Ph.D.

★ Part of your research will be to make an assessment of how much it is going to cost you to achieve your goals. I hope you have already been saving for a rainy day. Now it's time you start putting money aside for a sunny one.

★ Explore all the possible ways for you to work off your tuition or training. Surf the net. Visit the library. Talk to friends and acquaintances about funding sources. Look for creative financing. Are there scholarships, fellowships, and internships that may help you get your foot in the door? What can you do about setting up an informal apprenticeship program? An internship at a radio station that paid minimum wage put me on my path.

★ Do a line-by-line audit of what you are spending on a weekly basis and determine if your money is being used for maximum shine. Mark every expenditure with a plus or a minus. A minus would be cigarette purchases. A plus would be a year's membership at the gym. A minus would be processed food. A plus, fresh fruit. A minus, debts for things you haven't even worn since you brought them home from the dress store. A plus, tuition for chef's school you always dreamed of attending. What's your bottom line?

★ As you plan your budget consider that Hollywood producers believe in their projects so much that they often employ what's known as deficit spending. That means they will go into the first season of a television show knowing that they will be losing money for at least a year or more. They take the risk because if they have a hit, millions upon millions will follow. Make a similar commitment to wisely invest in your life. You, too, can hit the jackpot.

Storyboarding

Now that you have begun to make decisions on such issues as genre, setting, and budget it's time to do something else that comes up during the pre-production phase. It's called *storyboarding*. A storyboard is nothing more than a piece of paper with a series of panels of sketches that illustrate changes of scene and action. It's a blueprint. Storyboards help producers sort out the key scenes. Call it a visual aid for your visualization.

I saw the storyboards of director Alfred Hitchcock on display at New York's Museum of Modern Art and was amazed by the detail. Hitchcock was known to say that his storyboards were so elaborate that once they were completed he didn't even have to look in the camera lens to view his scenes because he knew exactly how they would turn out. Other filmmakers have followed his careful cues, including the creators of *The Matrix*. You think Keanu Reeves came up with those comic-book angles?

Draw your own key scenes on the worksheet called *Star Storyboard*. You can make stick figures as long as you can recognize the action. What kind of action, you ask? For example, as a college student my storyboard art would have included a panel of me on the first day of getting an internship at a radio station. Another one might have me doing a mock television newscast. And perhaps the final panel of the sequence would show me, in my sequined evening gown with a train, receiving an Emmy. Get it? Now do it. Write copy below the panels to describe what is going on during those scenes. If you're reading a book you've checked out from the library, start a notebook for your star excercises.

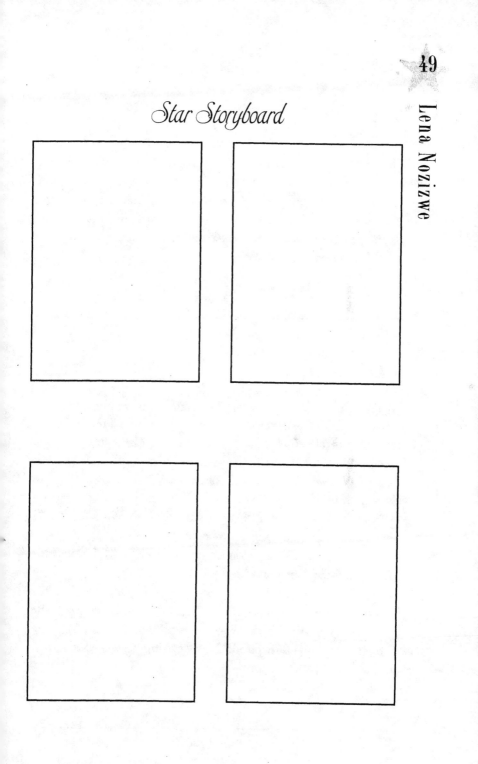

Star Storyboard

A Title for Your Role

I hope that seeing yourself in action inspired you to come up with a title for your starring role. Be creative. Draw from film titles that inspire you: *Mother Knows Best, My Years of Living Dangerously, When Sherry Met Pauly.* Brenda Smith, who attended my very first *Starring in Your Own Life* seminar, came up with the clever title *The Mominator.*

Star Title

Tagline

Next compose a *tagline.* A tagline is a descriptive phrase or sentence that describes the essence of your production. Here are some examples of effective ones. For the movie *Coffy* starring Pam Grier it was "The Baddest One-Chick Hit Squad That Ever Hit Town." *National Lampoon's Animal House* tagline was "We Can Do Anything We Want. We're College Students." For Harrison Ford's *Clear and Present Danger* it was "Truth Needs a Soldier." I don't have to spell out which movie this tagline is from: "The mob wanted Harlem back. They got Shaft up to here." That was for the original *Shaft,* by the way.

My student Brenda came up with her own clever tagline for *The Mominator.* "She cooks, she cleans, and the kids love her." She could have just as easily said that she was "The Baddest Mamma to Ever Hit Town." Inspired? Now it's time to write your own tagline.

Star Tagline

Photo

Take a photo of yourself in your starring role, make a copy, and paste it below. If you want to be an anchor, mock up a set in the living room. Get your brother to take the shot. If your dream is to be an astronaut, where can you pose near something spacey? If your next trip takes you to Washington, take the picture at the Smithsonian National Air and Space Museum. Your photo will just take your visualization a step further.

(Your Star Photo Here)

You can also videotape yourself in your starring role. You want to be a teacher? Videotape yourself as you pretend to teach in front of a classroom. Play the tape back for laughs and inspiration.

Poster

Creating a poster for a movie is challenging because you have to distill the very core of the production down to a single image. Now that you have your title, tagline, and genre figured out it's time for you to take that challenge. Use the worksheet with the heading *Starring* to concoct your creation.

Through the storyboarding process you have sorted through the key scenes. Now decide which one of those scenes is more important than any other. Will you be laughing out loud? Or will you be seriously contemplating the work at hand? Will there be costars in this poster? What will the setting be?

Again don't worry about how well you draw. We all can't be Norman Rockwells, Thomas Hart Bentons, or Al Hirschfelds, although all of the above created movie posters at one time or another in their illustrative careers.

The American Film Institute says the function of a poster has been to ". . . advertise and promote the film, but also to intrigue the imagination, glamorize the stars and pitch the Hollywood dream." That's a big job. Your own poster must do even more. It will pitch your dream.

After You've Filled in the Blanks

Still ahead for you and your star transformation are the casting process, editing, and happy endings. I'm getting ahead of myself because now that we have looked at the what of your starring role it's time to explore the whys.

★ ★ ★ ★ ★ ★ ★ ★ ★ ★ ★ ★ ★ ★ ★ ★ ★

Starring

(Your name here)

★ ★ ★ ★ ★ ★ ★ ★ ★ ★ ★ ★ ★ ★ ★ ★ ★

Ideals are like the stars. We never reach them,
but like the mariners on the sea,
we chart our course by them.
—CARL SCHURZ

★

CHAPTER THREE

What Is Your Motivation?

The Underlying Forces That Make You Glow

Television is supposed to be glamorous. Well, I was not feeling it
when I landed at BWI airport in Baltimore at one in the morning after a cross-country trip. I made the flight in connection with
a television appearance. Originally I had agreed to use vacation
time to take on the extracurricular project because I think highly
of the show producer. It seemed as though it might be fun. In addition the program itself was to benefit a worthy charity.

But I was dismayed when I saw that the show's producers
booked me on an airline I refer to as Moo Air. Why do I call it Moo
Air? Because from the boarding process through the flight, you
feel as though you are in steerage—that's a pun, I hasten to add.
My normal travel agent laughed when I told her my flight plans.

"Bring your own food," she advised. It was no joke. What was normally a five-and-a-half-hour flight stretched to eight uncomfortable hours, complete with two stopovers. And there was not much in the feedbag other than light snacks of crackers and maybe a carrot or two.

When I had first gotten wind of the arrangements, my instinct was to bail. After almost ten bicoastal years I know exactly how exhausting the flight can be under normal conditions. Not to mention that the early call time came barely four hours after my bleary-eyed arrival. It would make it close to impossible to shine for the show, which was really my job.

I was even more annoyed when I heard that my male counterpart was consulted and had been able to select his own flight on a non-Moo airline. The "fun" of the project was dissipating. It was time to take another look at why I was getting involved with the show in the first place. Time to check my motivation. I wasn't doing it for the money, which was nominal. It was not for the fame; the program had a limited cable audience. In the end the reason that I went on with the show was the fact that it was a good cause. The program spread the word about relief programs around the world, including in my homeland of Africa.

It has become a cliché for actors preparing for a scene to ask the director: "What is my motivation?" It's a question you must also consider as you prepare for your starring role. In a play or movie it's the character's motivation that makes her or him tick. If the script that you want to live out calls for you to do great things, you will need a great motivation. In the worst of times it may be the only thing that you'll be able to hang on to. Think of mountaineers whose lives depend on anchoring their climbing devices securely into jagged edges. They had better make sure they are hooked into solid ground because anything less and they can lose their footing and even their lives. A weak motivation can be equally perilous. The trick is to hook your life into solid motives and use them as your guide. Nietzsche said, "If we have our own 'why' of life we can bear almost any 'how.'"

Begin by asking yourself the obvious. What is your motivation? What is at the core of your starring role? Take time to focus on the forces that move you. You are likely to have more than one.

Go through a twenty-four-hour period and analyze your actions and the motivations behind them. Why do you get out of bed every morning? Is it so you can see the morning light? So you can look into the eyes of your loved ones? Why do you go to work? Is it just for the paycheck? Or is it because of the camaraderie you share? Do you really love what it is you do? Do you smile at the man at the gas station because you want to make sure he doesn't mess up your change? Or do you smile to cheer him because you see that he's having a troubled day? Do you go home to your husband and children every night because you can't figure out what else to do with your life? Or do you go home because you can't wait to be reunited with the people you love most? Of course your answers may change a bit from day to day. But this exercise may help you get to the core of what motivates your everyday life. After you have done that, dig deeper to determine what is the motivation behind your whole life.

Ultimately your heart and soul will determine the truth about your motivation. But check with your fans, costars, and supporting players. A former costar once told me that my motivation was fame. I listened but questioned his assessment, in part because when there was a choice between increasing screen time or expressing myself as a storyteller, the story always came first. I enjoy it so much that if I had stayed in Africa I would likely be sharing tales around a fire. But hearing this evaluation about my motivation made me stronger in my beliefs about what really mattered to me.

★ Greta Garbo admitted that money mattered a lot to her. The late actress said it was a big motivation behind prolonging her stay in the movie business. But she believed that it ruined her spiritually and made her subject to the whims of studio executives. If the number one motivation for your starring role is money, do a careful audit. How much is the money you are seeking really costing you? It's possible that you'll end up spending that money on everything from drugs to designer duds to make up for the radiance that is missing in your life. Too often these purchases will bring nothing more than false brilliance. So when you add and subtract the total costs, are you really coming out ahead? Better to make less and enjoy what you do more.

★ Use something I call mini-motives to start you on your way. Go ahead and lose weight for that wedding or high school reunion. Take that French class because someone laughed at the way you pronounced "faux pas." But in the long run the weight loss is beneficial and speaking another language is simply smart.

Get It Write

Once you have determined what motivates you, print it up. This is your mission statement. Tom Cruise, in his role as the title character in the movie *Jerry Maguire,* stays up all night to compose a twenty-five-page mission statement and prints it up. He even has a title for it: "A Suggestion for the Future." In it he says, "We must embrace what is still virginal about our enthusiasm, we must crack open the tight clenched fist and give back a little for the common good, we must simply be the best version of ourselves."

★ Once you've come up with your own mission statement, post a condensed version everywhere along the road of your mission. This condensed version is your motto. Write it on chalkboards. Embroider it on pillows. Type it on your screensaver. Write it in the slippery, squeaky condensation of your bathroom mirror. Incorporate your motto into your business cards or personal stationery. Refer to it every time you have a difficult or questionable life scene. The message doesn't have to be too preachy or too long. You can find some inspiration from the business world. Just how memorable is Nike's line "Just do it"? If you are an achiever you could try "Just did it." Disneyland uses the motto "Happiest place on earth." You might want to call chez vous "Happiest home on earth." The peppermint Altoids are known as "The curiously strong mint." You might be knows as "The curiously strong future doctor."

My Motto

★ Compose your voice mail with your motivation in mind. Inspire everyone who calls.

★ Put together a collection of books that are representative of your motivation: Bibles, biographies, inspirational books.

★ Compile quotes from these books that are consistent with your motivation. Find even more quotes by surfing the net.

Cues from Costars

★ One way to enlist support for your starring role is to look for others with similar motivations. Sharing your life stage with people who have very different values can be destructive. Say you're with people whose daily motivation is to obliterate the unhappiness of their workweek by getting blotto every night. Not good. If your coworkers are motivated to do something positive, their strength will serve to uplift you.

★ Knowing the motivations of those you are compelled to share screen time with will also help you reach for your star, starting with your boss. What floats her boat? Is she in it for the money? Recognition (aka fame)? Think about those motivations when you approach her for something you are striving for. Pepper your dialogue with the appropriate phrases. Suppose you want to try a new way of organizing the office and your boss is motivated by money. Emphasize how much money your plan will save. When talking with a boss motivated by recognition, talk a lot about how much the front office will be impressed by the change.

Guidepost

Focusing on your motivation can be miraculous. Find yours and it will act like the North Star, guiding you through the triumphs and tragedies of this life. It will be a certain harbor for anytime you walk in uncertainty. It will shine through the fog. When you use it as a target, everything else will fall into place.

But knowing your purpose is not the same as knowing how to get there, how to achieve it. So now it's time for you to get your acts together: Acts I, II, and III.

Words are vehicles that can transport us from
the drab sands to the dazzling stars.
— M. ROBERT SYME

★

CHAPTER FOUR

Your Long-Term Life Script

Strategies That Will See You Through Your Leading Role

You've settled down to watch or read a juicy mystery. The characters are intriguing, the plot enthralling. But there is no way you're going to sit through the whole thing. That's because you're the type of person who just has to fast-forward to the end to see how it all turns out. Perfect. Because the best way to get to your starring role is to start at "the end." Once you know what your conclusion will be you can start plotting the exact steps it will take to get you there.

It's not unlike my approach to telling a story for television. Before I go out and shoot I call a number of sources to find out about the lay of the land. I'll have a good idea of the best sound bites and the story structure. In other words I have a lot of answers before I ask a single question on camera. Of course, once I actually get on the scene, things may change. But unplanned scenarios just mean I have to adapt, improvise. But at least there's a place to start, a plan. That's also true in life.

In pre-production you have at least started figuring out *where* you want to go. Now is the time to commit your long-term plans to black and white in the form of what I've been calling a life script. It's a compilation of the real and dream scenes of your life. Compare it to having a shopping list. When you go to the grocery store you are likely to forget something if you don't bring your notes. If you don't have a list of what you want to get out of life, you are also likely to leave out the most important ingredients. What would you like to cook up for your life drama?

Getting into the Act

Acts are nothing more than a sequence of scenes organized into distinct sections. As you write your long-term life script I would like you to divide those distinct sections into three acts following the model first used by the Greek philosopher Aristotle. Before there were $100 million-dollar blockbusters there were Greek plays, and Aristotle believed the most effective drama had a beginning, middle, and end.

To this day screenwriters follow that same structure. Check out how many movies you have seen recently where a story begins with an introduction of the main character, followed by scenes where the protagonist encounters complications as she goes toward her goals. And finally the resolution. Using that archetype separate your life script into where you are now (Act I), how you're going to get there (Act II), and exactly where it is that you want to go (Act III).

Act III

As you chart your plot, begin with the end. Exactly how do you want your Act III to play out when you have succeeded in your starring role? Using the worksheet labeled *Star Act III,* write down a climactic scene of this joyful act. Think about what would be included in the peak scene of your A&E *Biography* or MTV *BIOrhythm.* Don't hold back. This is the time to let your dreams flow as you weave your costars, setting, wardrobe, and dialogue into one fantastic scene. Describe it down to the room temperature and the music that will be playing in the background.

Let's say your starring role is becoming a kindergarten teacher. Perhaps for your Act III you want to describe how you will feel when you become teacher of the year because you have created a program that inspires the creativity of your students. What will your first words be as you accept your award? What will it be like to be faced with a crowd of fans, including your small charges? Imagine the sense of accomplishment you will feel for having made such a difference in the lives of children. Write down all of your musings. Of course to get there it means you have already done research for this role during pre-production so you have a sense of the life you will be living. If you're thinking, "I don't have a clue," it may be that you did not spend enough time in pre-production.

★ When you've finished your Act III, attach a deadline to your dream and keep it. Beware if your deadlines are lapsing with regularity; reexamine your goals. Maybe your starring role needs some changes. Or perhaps it's just going to take a longer time to achieve it and you have to dig in your heels. If you are feeling discouraged, just think that even after the success of *Driving Miss Daisy* it took the producers of the Oscar-winning movie seventeen years to bring the blockbuster *Deep Impact* to the screen. They just kept pitching. They kept going because of a strong belief in the concept.

★ One of the exciting things about your life script is that you really don't know exactly the time of *The* very *End*. So once you have achieved Act III, you have a chance to do it all again by expanding your role with a new dream, a new Act III. That future teacher of the year may think next about becoming a school administrator, and then maybe a school board member. As personal trainer to the stars Radu says, "Each success engenders a new goal."

★ ★ ★ ★ ★ ★ ★ ★ ★ ★ ★ ★ ★ ★ ★ ★

Star Act III

Coming to a life near you on (date) _____

★ ★ ★ ★ ★ ★ ★ ★ ★ ★ ★ ★ ★ ★ ★ ★

Act I

Now that you are done with Act III jump back to Act I. On the worksheet titled *Star Act I* make an honest assessment of where you are today. Do a character breakdown of you. List things like your age, where you live, and what you are doing with your life at this moment. I'm looking for a thumbnail description here. It's akin to a physical and psychological Polaroid. Get the picture?

You might begin with something like: *Twenty-something drifter in California who now works in fast food who is searching for something more . . . ambitious thirty-something in New England who made the wrong career choice and now wants to reinvent herself . . . forty-something success story living in Detroit looking for ways to slow down and enjoy life more . . . fifty-something Texan who is tired of regretting what might have been and now looks to what will be.*

Don't just include the good in this act, or the bad for that matter. Act I should simply be an honest overview. When you are finished, write clearly and succinctly what it is that is propelling you toward your goal, under the heading of *Turning Point,* also known by screenwriters as plot points. Then date it. A turning point might be that you broke up with your boyfriend who never wanted you to leave his side. Now that the two of you are apart you have decided that you will become a veterinarian, as you always wanted. Or it could be your plot point is that you have awoken from a blackout for the last time. Not only do you want to stop drinking, but also to stop waitressing and start training to be a computer software developer.

★ If it's hard for you to make an assessment of your current life think about how you would be described if you were a character on a TV show. Are you more *Roseanne* than *The Nanny?* More like one of the *Friends* than one of the *Simpsons?*

★ If you are still having trouble, see if your friends and family can help fill in a few strokes. You may not even realize how you have been acting out your current role.

★ ★ ★ ★ ★ ★ ★ ★ ★ ★ ★ ★ ★ ★ ★ ★

Star Act 1

Turning point

Today's date_____

★ ★ ★ ★ ★ ★ ★ ★ ★ ★ ★ ★ ★ ★ ★ ★ ★

Act II

Act II literally comes between reality and your dreams. It's where the real work comes in. If you want to become a movie star, Act II is where you actually audition for movies. Or it's starting your innovative art program for kids as you go toward becoming teacher of the year. In this act list all of the steps you must take, which might include: getting invitations to movie screenings so you can meet with producers, or getting the supplies from an art store for your program, and so on.

Write all of that down on the worksheet titled *Star Act II*.

Many of us want to skip this act and go from waitress to Oscar winner, but this is where real character development comes in; it's in Act II where you will encounter real-life plot twists that will threaten to keep you from achieving your Act III. The plot will thicken with what screenwriters call complications or escalating events.

Since you know it's coming include a list of every possible crisis you may encounter and how you plan to take it on under the headings of *Obstacles* and *Solutions* on the *Star Act II* worksheet. For example, let's go back to that goal of creating a special program for your kids and then becoming a stellar teacher. Let's say you can't afford to run the program. What are your options? Taking a second job? Getting a grant? Being aware of all of your options and solutions will help make your journey less intimidating.

★ Look closely at those obstacles. Do you see any patterns? Are some of them of your own making? Perhaps you have more control over them than you think.

★ In spite of the challenges you'll encounter in Act II, make it an inextricable part of your life script to have fun along the way. If you have to take that second job, make sure that you play your favorite song every day before you get to work. If you go for a grant, make friends with the charity. Not because you want to ingratiate yourself but because you want to make the process of getting help fun. You can look forward to even more advice in chapter 5 about finding joy along the way to your Act III.

★ ★ ★ ★ ★ ★ ★ ★ ★ ★ ★ ★ ★ ★ ★ ★

Star Act II

Obstacles   Solutions

★ ★ ★ ★ ★ ★ ★ ★ ★ ★ ★ ★ ★ ★ ★ ★

> Make a picture of your route to success. First visualize
> the journey of getting from here to there. Draw a
> point on one side of your piece of paper to indicate
> where you are now. Then draw a star on the other side
> to represent where you are going. In the middle,
> sketch possible roadblocks, using the symbol of an ac-
> tual roadblock. Then imagine suitable detours.
>
> ★

Backstage Jitters

Imagine a chef with a collection of fabulous recipes she never con-
cocts. A musician storing a trove of melodies that are never
played. Or a gardener with a bountiful stash of heirloom seeds
that are never sown. It's the same thing if you create a starring role
you never bring to life.

Fear plays a big part in keeping us from hitting the stage. As
African statesman Nelson Mandela said so brilliantly, "Our worst
fear is that we are powerful beyond measure. It is our light, not
our darkness that most frightens us. We ask ourselves, 'Who am I
to be brilliant, gorgeous, talented and fabulous?' Actually, who
are you not to be?"

In Hollywood there are thousands of scripts that are never produced. But the best movie story is meaningless if it languishes in a
drawer gathering dust. As I look around me I see evidence of
countless dream lives that have never been produced. That you
have written a script for your life, no matter how exciting and fulfilling it may be, means absolutely nothing if you don't bring it to
life. You've written it. Shake off the stage fright. Begin to live your
life script. It's time for the director (that would be you) to yell "action!"

★ How do you make sure your dreams avoid dust bunnies? For one thing, make sure you've written a life script that really suits you. How good do you feel when you are visualizing the scenes of Act III? Do you crave it? When it came to casting TV shows, the late NBC programmer Brandon Tartikoff said ". . . if an actor doesn't seem to want the role badly enough at the onset, the arrangement rarely works." It's not going to work as you act out your life script either. You should positively glow when you think about it. If not, review, revise, and reconsider.

★ Take every opportunity to bring your role into action. If you want to be a teacher, teach at your church. If you want to be a chef, make your personal meals stellar. If you want to write, fill every note to your mother with bons mots.

★ Recognize any unexpected opportunity that unfolds that can propel you to your starring role. Fran Drescher really wanted her own show. She had been working on a series called *Princesses* for CBS. That show was not long for the world, when she took off for France. The head of CBS happened to be on her plane during her route back. Fran admits she looked a mess that day but it did not stop her. She went into the bathroom and pulled herself together. She kept repeating to herself, "carpe diem," which you may remember from the movie *Dead Poets Society* means seize the day. She seized the day all right by engaging Jeff Sagansky, then the CBS network president, in a conversation. Before she got off the plane she convinced him to schedule a pitch meeting. That begat the television series *The Nanny*.

★ Find support groups comprised of people who share similar goals. For a farmer it would be Future Farmers of America. Are there any classes that keep your eyes on the prize? Make those courses positive and constant reinforcement.

★ If you have stage fright because you think you are too old to take on a starring role remember the late Walter Matthau's words in the movie *Out to Sea*. "There is no such thing as too late. That's why they invented death."

Although your life script is designed to be inspiring, it can also be a daunting piece of work. But remember as I said earlier, the best roles are the most demanding. If you are a bit overwhelmed by the big picture, you can start shining brighter right now by making simple changes in your day-to-day life.

> Those who look up see the stars.
> —SOUTHERN PROVERB

★

CHAPTER FIVE

Your Short-Term Life Script

Shine This Instant

★ ★ ★ ★ ★ ★ ★ ★ ★ ★ ★ ★ ★ ★ ★ ★ ★

FADE UP FROM BLACK

INT. COMFORTABLE BEDROOM—DOMINATED BY BLACK AND SILVER GOTHIC BED—DAY
DISSOLVE TO: Refreshed Woman awakes after a night of untroubled sleep on her extra-firm queen-size bed. She languishes for a moment, savoring the beauty of her silky, color-coordinated bed linens.

REFRESHED WOMAN
"Ahhhhhhhhh." (She sighs contentedly.)

INT. BATHROOM—FILLED WITH CANDLES, SOAPS, AND ARTWORK COLLECTED FROM AROUND THE WORLD—DAY

DISSOLVE TO: Refreshed Woman walks to golden and perfumed bathroom, her silk negligee billowing behind her. She begins running her bubble bath. Ritualistically she lights up the fragrant candles that surround her bath and steps into the water. She savors these moments of relaxation before she must head out the door.

RELAXED WOMAN
"Ahhhhhhhhhhhhhhhhhhhhhhhhhhhh." (She sighs contentedly.)

★ ★ ★ ★ ★ ★ ★ ★ ★ ★ ★ ★ ★ ★ ★ ★ ★

I cast myself in the role of the refreshed and relaxed woman. Though I may not be able to control what happens in my workday, both you and I can set the stage for a good morning, almost every morning. It's not unlike planning a camera shoot. A few summers ago I worked with a delightful local crew in the tiny village of Benest in southwest France. Since this was France, I wanted a particular shot to include a checkered tablecloth, a blooming bougainvillea, and a crusty baguette. Olivier, one of my French colleagues, was bemused by all the effort I went to for a tableau that would only be on-camera for a matter of seconds. He called it my mise-en-scène. What sort of daily life script do you wake up to? If your personal mise-en-scène includes scenes like "My yellowing, hole-infested, ratty nightshirt billows behind me," it's time for a rewrite.

Playing Daily

Every day the sun comes up a curtain also rises on a whole new series of scenes just waiting for you to act them out. In the last chapter, we talked about writing a comprehensive overview of the life you desire. Well, getting to Act III takes time. Right now you may not be at the location you desire or with the costars you dream of, or acting out your fantasy role (although I hope that by now you are starting to prepare). The good news is that every day offers you a precious opportunity to write, produce, and execute lines for happy interludes for the recurring scenes of your life. Scenes you can act out today, immediately, right this very minute.

Wake Up

★ Stage direct your morning wake-up. Create a personal mise-en-scène that encompasses all of your senses, starting with sight. What's the first thing you see in the morning? A loving spouse is not a bad place to start. Another way to gently wake your senses is to position a flowering plant in a beautiful container in your direct line of view.

★ Instead of getting up to the blaring sound of an alarm clock, tune your radio to a classical music station. Another alternative is a device that increases the intensity of light to get you out of bed. There's another alarm on the market that shakes and vibrates you awake. An aromatherapy alarm uses infusions of fragrance. I just heard about an affirmation clock that greets you with encouraging words that you record such as "I am a superstar," or "I am wonderful."

★ Speaking of dialogue, what words normally start your day? When preparing for an interview with Kathleen Ford, the widow of Henry Ford II in Palm Beach, I came across a phrase he used to greet the day. The scion of an automotive dynasty would reportedly look in the mirror and say, "I am the king and the king can do no wrong." Sharon Y. Cobb says she starts every morning with an affirmation that she will become a more successful screenwriter. Her intentions are more than just words. Peacemaker Mahatma Gandhi said,

"Language is an exact reflection of the character and growth of its speakers."

★ Make the first thing you touch every morning silky, velvety, fleecy, or plush. It can be your sheets, your lingerie, or slippers. If it feels good, touch it.

★ Place a bowl of potpourri, within nose range, next to your bed.

★ Have a full menu of bubble bath on tap. There are so many varieties available today. Take your pick if you want to take one that calms or invigorates you. As you are soaking, just think that there was a scene in the 1932 film *The Sign of the Cross* showing Claudette Colbert soaking in asses' milk that historians say prompted the beginning of the bubble bath industry.

★ You may have seen those plastic headrests for your tub. For a more luxe look and feel, get one in terry cloth. I found one on sale at an outlet.

★ Think about the things you taste every morning. I'm not just talking about breakfast. What about the flavor of your toothpaste and mouthwash? Consult with your dentist to make sure your selection keeps your teeth sparkling.

★ As you brush your teeth or take that bubble bath, plot out the scenes of how you would like your dream day to go. Tell yourself what a wonderful day you will have. Then go about making that come true.

★ Program your life for joy by using pass codes, such as joy, bliss, or happiness for your ATM card or voice mail. Feel that way whenever you punch in your code.

★ Reading from a daily devotional is one way of insuring that divine light will guide you. There are many on the market designed to compliment all kinds of lifestyles.

★ Every morning when singer and actress Dolly Parton gets up, she says she visualizes God picking her up by the heels and "holding me upside down until all of the bad, negative things fall out into that circle of light." She says God then stands her up and she imagines light filling her until she becomes "a being of light." Start your day in a similar positive light.

Weekly Script

Every week you take your garbage out for the trash man, you get your pedicure, and you get your weekly subscription to *Punk World*. Add weekly pleasures to that schedule that is already filling with daily delights. These events may be more elaborate than what you plan for every day. It may mean taking a special trip, as I did when I chased my favorite hip-hop teacher across town every weekend in order to take his class. But it was just one weekly excursion I could look forward to that would bring me joy.

★ Design your life so that you always have something to look forward to. As I write this I am looking forward to going to the prime-time Emmys with my family. Then I am looking forward to going to Germany for the first time for an international book fair. Your feel-good schedule does not have to be so far-flung, but next month schedule in a visit to your favorite garden that's an hour outside of the city. The following month look forward to going to that play that everyone is talking about. Now when you look at your calendar you have reasons to smile. If you get invited to even more events, great. You already have a place to start.

★ Television stations often promote theme weeks: bad-girl week, Denzel Washington week, and so on. From time to time schedule special weeks on your personal calendar. For example, you could have flower week where you surround yourself in blooms. Spread the petal power around your office. You don't have to spend a fortune. Maybe you can go out and pick some wildflowers. An avid gardener friend might be tickled to share some flowers.

Facing a Bad Day

You made a mistake. You missed a deadline. You tussled with the boss's pet. Now it's time to face the music. We all have bad days. But plot your daily life script in advance so that you know exactly how you are going to handle the inevitable. On these days you'll need an extra cushion of radiance in place to keep you going. Plan on it.

When you know it's going to be a rough one make sure that before you go to work that you've already had a stellar morning . . . the gentle alarm clock, the silky pajamas, and the devotional. Pay special care putting yourself together. Wear something that guarantees compliments and be sure to put on a smile. I suggest that you keep repeating this dialogue over and over again in your head: "I am a winner—a star, even if I made a mistake." Don't typecast yourself as a loser just because of your blunder. Then go forth with as much grace as possible.

★ Somehow make sure that your dialogue on that bad day includes the message that things will get better. Also keep telling yourself that no matter how bad the event is that is unfolding in your life, you are good.

★ Smile. Some studies have shown that fake smiles can produce real happiness. Researchers say that smiling causes us to feel

better because the action pumps up the production of serotonin and dopamine, brain chemicals that make us feel good.

★ Step outside your role and do something for others, immediately. Buy lunch for a homeless person you encounter on
the street (that is if you feel safe doing so). Go through your
closets and collect items to donate to charity. Be moved by a
news story about someone who needs help. Reaching out to
someone less fortunate can be an amazingly swift way of
getting beyond that "poor, pitiful me" life script. Studies at
Columbia University show that doing good increases the
release of that feel-good chemical dopamine.

★ One of the best pick-me-ups I know of is new underwear.
When I'm having a bad day I wear the silkiest and laciest I
can find. We're not talking about La Perla; in fact, I have
bought some of my favorites at discount stores for less than
five dollars. You can never have too many.

★ Reach for the stars. Literally. An Ohio State University
psychologist says raising your arms is a way of beating the
blues. He thinks it is because flexing your arms is an action
you take when you eat. An activity many of us enjoy too
much. But this way there are no extra calories.

★ Create a personalized list of five things you will do the next
time you are not feeling so great. Reach for it and go on auto-
matic pilot when you get in a bad mood.

★ Aggressively look for something to do. Something you can
control. Something that you can do well. Something that
you can accomplish without the slightest chance of failure.
Bake a cake. Paint a chair. Prune a rose bush. When you
have completed that assignment give yourself a high
five.

★ Get a massage. Studies show that if you get rubbed the right way you can reduce stress hormones. Best-selling self-help author Dr. Harold Bloomfield says he actually recommends massage for patients with low-level depression.

★ Maybe you can't afford to cheer yourself up with a whole bouquet, so spend a couple of bucks for one beautiful bloom.

★ Be daring. Call that Ms. Big you have been afraid to approach. Submit that article for possible publication. Put in that application for your dream job. You are already feeling as though you are at the bottom so if you are shot down so what? Move on.

When You Are Having a Great Day

★ A great day is also the perfect time to go outside the boundaries of your comfort zone. Go for the outrageous when you are basking in the glow of success. When you're hot turn the heat on even higher for even more accomplishments.

★ Deal with daunting tasks on this day. Your success will make your challenges seem less intimidating.

★ Commit to memory all the nuances of the goodness of your good day so you can replay it when things are not going so well.

Preparing for an Important Meeting

Diva Diana Ross says before she has an important meeting she will visualize the entire exchange from beginning to end. Then she considers all of the possibilities of what will happen. That way she is prepared for whatever may come. When he began living la vida loca singing sensation Ricky Martin went over the possible questions journalists would ask with veteran performer Gloria Estefan. If these stars still prepare for important meetings, why can't you?

★ If possible, go to the location early—even the day before. That way you don't have to scramble the day of and you'll look as though you belong in the setting.

★ Find out as much as you can about the set design of your all-important meeting. Then think about ways of adding sparkle to your appearance. If the room is dark, you may want to stand out by wearing light and bright colors. Or vice versa. If the setting is industrial and cold, think of ways of bringing warmth inside.

★ Do a dress rehearsal the night before. Try on what you are going to be wearing, from head to toe. Don't wear the black pumps with the heel that's run-down. Forget about those off-black stockings with the little snag. Don't even think about using a safety pin to fix that gaping hem. Better to find out those wardrobe problems in previews. Fix it or wear something else.

★ Examine what your outfit will look like in lighting that mimics your meeting place. It's funny but sometimes a dress will look perfectly fine at home, but when you are out in direct sunlight it looks spotted. You don't want to make that kind of fashion statement unless you are wearing a leopard print.

★ Will the person you are meeting with see you mostly above the waist or will they get a full-body view? If you'll be seen mostly above the waist, think in terms of television anchors who concentrate on what the audience sees. That means attention to necklines, scarves, and shoulders. If you were to go behind the scenes of some television news sets you would see jeans and even shorts. If the person you are meeting with will see a full-body view, forget about a wraparound or split skirt or you may act out a scene from a movie I'll call *Indecent Exposure*.

★ I was reminded of how critical your point of view can be at a televised awards show. Cohost Jenna Elfman got a fair amount of criticism for the dress she was wearing. Above the waist the dress was pleasant enough. In person, however, it looked stunning. At home you could not see the fabulous fishtail hem.

Coming Home

★ Hollywood stars may have butlers and maids to greet them when they come home. Be your own Jeeves. Before going to work, put out your fuzzy, warm slippers and silky lounging pajamas.

★ As you go out the door in the morning, spray a whiff of your favorite fragrance in your entryway so it will greet you upon your return. My favorite home scent is Cote Bastide's fig perfume.

★ If you live alone set your timer so the lights come on just before you return home. That way you won't be returning to a dark, dismal living space.

★ Have a wonderful treat awaiting you. Maybe a bowl of strawberries arranged in a silver bowl. Or perhaps some bonbons (nonfat of course). All day long you'll know that guilty pleasure awaits you.

★ Make sure the last thing you see before you close your eyes to sleep is upbeat. A scary movie or a bullet-riddled newscast is not the ticket.

★ Actress Lana Turner said it was a bad day if she did not laugh at least three times. If you are feeling blue on your way home, my prescription is to rent two comedies and call me in the morning. Once you get home, pop some corn and laugh.

Writing Your Own Daily Scenes

I hope that my suggestions have given you some ideas about the creation of your very own daily life script. Of course, you may have to make some adjustments. Perhaps you work the night shift, or you work as an at-home mom, or maybe travel makes your schedule erratic. No problem. With some minor modifications you can expand your stellar scenes. The important thing is to get into a rhythm of injecting maximum star power into your everyday life.

I've created some short-term life script worksheets designed to help you personalize your best day. Begin by describing the setting, be it interior (INT) or exterior (EXT), of where your scenes are taking place. Unlike the long-term life script where you focus on your dreams and the steps needed to achieve them, your short-term life script is comprised of what is in your life right here and right now. But don't forget that it is possible to make immediate improvements. For example, if part of your current setting includes dirty, wrinkled sheets, clean and iron them so you can describe a scene that includes fluffy, fresh-smelling linen.

Again the key is to write the scenes according to what you can do immediately. If it is not realistic for you to take the time for a bubble bath, then write your daily life script so that you begin your day with a fresh-smelling shower gel. If little ones make it impossible for you to light up candles then turn on a soft pink light in the bathroom as you get ready. Growing flowers may be out of the question. Then plan to feast your eyes on a painting of the same.

As you fill in the dialogue think about the words you would like to say every day. What about a prayerful "Thank you God for giving me another day" or an "I love you" to your romantic lead? And remember this is your dialogue, not anyone else's. It's what you have control of in your day. As for sound effects write in the music or any other sounds you would like to be surrounded by.

Start with at least two scenes of how you would like to begin and end your days. Act on them today!

The next time someone tells you to "have a nice day" you will now have a script on hand to ensure that you can do exactly that. And although I would like you to be consistent in acting out your optimum daily life script, don't beat yourself up if you can't do it every single day. On occasion writing, shooting, and traveling have forced me to make changes. That's just how it goes. You have to remember the whole purpose of this scripting session is to illuminate your life, not to make you crazy.

Once you have written them it will be easy enough to commit these scenes to memory. But keep your written copy handy because it's helpful to refer to it every now and then. Don't hesitate to revise your life script when you come up with even better ideas. And as you'll find out in the next chapter, one way you can really make your scripts sparkle is by editing.

★ ★ ★ ★ ★ ★ ★ ★ ★ ★ ★ ★ ★ ★ ★ ★ ★

_____'s *Daily Life Script:*
Morning

FADE UP FROM BLACK

INT OR EXT:

DISSOLVE TO:

DIALOGUE/SOUND EFFECTS

★ ★ ★ ★ ★ ★ ★ ★ ★ ★ ★ ★ ★ ★ ★ ★ ★

* * * * * * * * * * * * * * * * *

_____'s *Daily Life Script:*
Evening

FADE UP FROM BLACK

INT OR EXT:

DISSOLVE TO:

DIALOGUE/SOUND EFFECTS

* * * * * * * * * * * * * * * * *

No one regards what is before his feet;
we all gaze at the stars.
—Quintus Ennius

★

CHAPTER SIX

Editing

Cut Judiciously to Enhance Your Shine

As a diamond gets chipped away it becomes more brilliant, until it is pared down to its essential most dazzling form. The skill of a diamond cutter will transform a dull rock into a jewel that becomes its best and brightest. The excess is swept away. Then the polishing begins.

The same concept goes into putting together a television segment. A five-minute story might represent hours of videotape. I have always been more than willing to go an extra hour for an interview even if it means coming up with no more than a powerful fifteen-second sound bite. After gathering all the material for a story, I sit with an editor and together we cut away all the excess in order to uncover the most dazzling story. Quite often it's that fifteen seconds that will make a story shine.

Hollywood well knows how much editing can affect a production. That's why filmmakers fight for the right to have the final cut. When they do not have control directors have been known to ask that their names be taken off the credits.

Titanic director, James Cameron, was none too pleased when he got word that the producers of his first film, *Piranha 2: The Spawning,* edited the film without him. As the story goes he was so determined to have it cut to his liking that he flew to Rome and broke into the editing room. At the time he had no food, no money, and he was sick. In addition the future Oscar winner was not so familiar with the Italian editing equipment. Even so he proceeded to recut the film just the way he wanted it.

Our lives are filled with a kaleidoscope of scenes, good, bad, and ugly. When you think about it you'll realize that you have been editing them. You can't remember everything. Perhaps you recall your sixth birthday party. But the ninth is a bit fuzzy. You know you fell for a cute counselor at summer camp, but you cannot remember the name of the boy you had a crush on during the regular school year.

I have sat many times in an editing room with boxes of tapes and put together a television segment. Editing your life is more like editing a live event, where a director cuts from camera to camera to capture the best action. So it's up to you to cut from scene to scene; you will find some that you only want to last seconds and some that you don't even want to "take" at all.

As the producer-director of your star vehicle you get to decide what ends up on the cutting room floor. Instead of recalling a hodgepodge of memories, why not use judicious editing to concentrate on the best of everything. Think Tina Turner. She said that when she left her abusive husband, Ike, she threw all of those memories "in a trash can." Linger on the scenes of accomplishment, love, and joy. Trim those filled with self-doubt, self-destruction, and self-loathing.

★ Analyze a day of your rushes (the raw scenes) and consider content. Let's say you have already determined that your starring role means that you must further your education. Yet somehow when you look at your day it seems that you are spending most of your time just maintaining and not reaching for the stars. Tomorrow edit your schedule accordingly so you devote at least a portion of your time to education. That could mean something as simple as ordering a class schedule or calling up a friend of a friend who is a teacher.

★ As you look at those daily rushes, also think about the pacing of your day. Does it resemble a frenetically cut music video, when you would prefer it to be more along the lines of the slow rhythm of a nature series? Look for ways to alter your speed. Adjusting your pacing can make you feel supremely serene or actively alive.

★ When I am struggling with a decision, there is a quick edit guide I use. I ask myself, will doing this make me wiser? Will it make me more beautiful, inside or out? Will it enrich me? By the way, I didn't say, "Will this make me richer?" I also ask, "Will it bring me closer to God?" If I say no to all of the above, I seriously have to consider pushing the edit button.

★ Director Alfred Hitchcock was a master at shooting a scene from a variety of different angles. Then he cut together an exciting sequence. When you are putting together a real-life scene, consider all of the angles. Look at it from a bird's-eye view; in other words look at the overall picture of what the decision will mean to your life. Consider it from a dog's-eye view. That means reflecting on what your choice will mean in the down and dirtiest terms. Or look at it close up where you see minute details, pores and all. Contemplate your navel. If you can't see the virtue of that upcoming scene after reviewing every angle, cut to the next one.

Dialogue

★ There are words that simply don't belong in your life script. You might think the words are benign, kinda funny, or inconsequential, but remember that words define us. Never refer to yourself with such words as "stupid," "dummy," "idiot." I've used those words when I misplaced something but it sure didn't help me find it any faster. I simply could have called myself "forgetful." Can you think of a reason why you would use any of those names? They are words that are *never* appropriate for children or anyone else you love.

★ There are some other phrases that don't belong in your dialogue. Edit the following: "... would have ... ," "... should have ... ," "... could have." *Just do it!* Edit "I can't." Substitute *you can!* If you are saying, "I'm not smart enough," "I'm not pretty enough," "I'm not good enough," *yes you are!*

★ Diana Ross says she listens to see if criticism of her focuses on how she looks or on being too old or too young. If it does she simply edits those comments. Good advice.

★ See how often you can replace the words "I'll try" with "I will" in your conversations.

★ Even before she took time off, singer Celine Dion has been known, when on tour, to protect her golden vocal chords between performances by not speaking. Periodically become a diva by editing all of your dialogue for a day. Fill in your family in advance so they don't think you're crazy. Use the twenty-four hours to keep your mouth shut and really listen to what others have to say.

In with the Good

★ If you need help accentuating the positive, think of the people who compose newspaper advertisements for movies. They must take a review and extract the best quotes. Sometimes it's a real stretch to find something nice, but they do. It can be just a word. The next time you catch yourself dwelling on the negative, think of those ads and of ways you can glean the most glowing quotes.

★ Your motivation can serve as your edit guide. It will help you figure out what in your life is worth keeping and what you can toss. After being overwhelmed with a schedule that had her going to several meetings and screenings a day, screenwriter Sharon Y. Cobb says she came up with a sort of caller ID (you know, that feature on your phone that tells you who is calling before you pick it up). She says it enables her to sort out which invitations and activities are time wasters and which will help her toward her goal. Work on your ability to see the difference between the wheat and the chaff.

★ Put the good stuff in rewind. Diva Diana Ross does. When she is battling negative thoughts she will often turn on her tape recorder and play a previous show to remind herself of her own uplifting words. She also carries around a library of inspirational tapes. Record your triumphs and tote them around with you to replay whenever you need a lift. If you have a video camera that can work, too. I'm finding that I reread my own book for inspiration.

Out with the Bad

Enough with the rewinding of the unpleasant scenes and dialogue from your life. I have been guilty of dwelling on the negative and not paying enough attention to the many wonderful scenes that have played out in my life. The next time you catch yourself doing that, say, "Enough already." Mentally press the stop button. Fast-forward to the happier future you've been creating in your mind.

★ Write down your most troubling worries. Once you are finished, shred them. Feel better. Then figure out how you can really rip those problems from out of your life.

★ Do you feel drained after reading or watching what's supposed to be entertainment? Edit. In his book *8 Weeks to Optimum Health,* Dr. Andrew Weil recommends going on news fasts. That means cutting the often-depressing evening news out of your daily viewing diet. Even the Surgeon General has supported a prescription of reducing television viewing. While you're at it cut out other negative content in media such as video games and movies.

★ They say what you think about grows larger. So that means you should immediately stop thinking about your rear end. What else needs pruning?

Cut! Print!

Actively and thoughtfully shaping the scenes of your life separates the stars from the spectators. It forces you to become more attuned to what's good for you, to what makes you shine. It means you are tailoring your life to suit you and only you. And don't forget that plants that are trimmed flourish more than those left uncut.

The ability to edit means just one more opportunity to take control of your life. One area that can always benefit from nips and tucks is the people with whom you share the spotlight, your costars.

Hitch your wagon to a star.
— RALPH WALDO EMERSON

★

CHAPTER SEVEN

Costars, Supporting Players, Fans, and Villains

Increase Your Star Power Through Casting

Life will never be a one-woman show. It's an ever-changing ensemble of costars, supporting players, extras, fans, and, yes, villains. The cast of characters in our lives impacts us in profound ways. I am reminded of just how big a role they have every time I sort out my laundry. If I were to mix white lingerie with a red leotard I'd end up with pink undergarments. The people in your life can leave behind similar residue. How are the players in your life affecting your true colors? If they are not adding sparkle, it's time to sort them out.

Your cast can do one of two things. They can help you shine or they diminish your luster. Start today to fill your scenes with the best and brightest.

Costars

Casting directors will see hundreds and even thousands of hopefuls before they cast a single role. They're looking for acting talent, particular physical types, and that elusive chemistry. You want to see an example of good chemistry look at any movie with Katharine Hepburn and Spencer Tracy.

After attending a British Motion Picture Academy screening of the autobiographical movie *Angela's Ashes,* director Alan Parker amazed me when he said the production considered some fifteen thousand boys to play the roles of lead Frank McCourt and his siblings. Movie types take all that trouble and expense to cast well because it has such an enormous impact on the outcome of a production. How much effort do you go through selecting the people you share your life with?

Starring in your own life means actively selecting costars as a conscious choice rather than letting people simply drift into your life.

When casting works in Hollywood you can see it onscreen and off. I keep running into the cast members of *Fresh Prince of Bel-Air,* whom I've seen hanging out together everywhere, from my exercise classes to the neighborhood of my favorite Los Angeles hotel. Mind you the show has not been in production for years. Great casting.

The casting was not so good for a local anchor team I know that was so competitive it would analyze news scripts not for content, but to see who had the most lines. How can you dazzle with costars like that?

In another example a female anchor thought she had found her starring role in a major market. But she told me the first night she sat with her male coanchor he grumpily commented that she looked taller than he did on the monitor. "Do something about lowering your chair," he huffed. It got worse. This anchor said management later came to her with a request for her to intentionally flub her words every now and then so her less-than-perfect male counterpart, who was known to take a nip of the sauce every now and then, wouldn't look so bad. As you might expect she did not last at the station very long. The last time I heard she had a job in a smaller market with a smaller paycheck but she was able to put a bigger portion of her star power on display. Her new costars are more supportive.

Be careful about being so impressed by the possibility of a new job or a new relationship that you don't consider whom your new costars will be. Don't put yourself in a situation where you are forced to hide your light under a bushel.

Who Will Be Sharing the Bill?

I was able to let it shine, let it shine, let it shine when I worked in San Diego in local news. I made a lot of appearances on the early afternoon show. Every time I stepped out onto the set with newsman Hal Clement I always felt that I would do better just being in his presence. He always made me feel very comfortable. Unlike my colleague who went to the major market, when I sat side by side with Hal I knew he wanted me to shine. And he was so good at his craft that it inspired me to do better.

A par golfer friend of mine who labors on the links of Palm Beach and Toronto tells me that he prefers to play with golfers who are better than he is. That's how he gets better. You can also get better by playing in the leagues of men and women who go toward the light.

When my former production assistant, Cathy Stanley, became a successful producer for BET (Black Entertainment Television), no one could be prouder of her than I was. When my book agent, Jenny Bent, made a deal so spectacular it was written up in trade publications, I was buzzed. When screenwriter Sharon Y. Cobb sold her script to 20th Century-Fox, I was so excited for her. I find great inspiration when people around me do well. If you still find yourself feeling a bit envious, turn that angst into what I call creative jealousy. Use the success of others to open your eyes to the possibilities of what you can do. Revel in the good tidings of your costars. It's so much more constructive than begrudging their accomplishments. Take a cue from Oprah Winfrey's costar and best friend Gayle King, who says, "I never feel I'm in her shadow," she says, "I feel like I'm in her light. . . ."

Sometimes the most important support a costar can give you has her poised just out of the spotlight. Movie and television director Tracy Britton says Heather Locklear is that way. Tracy tells me she was working on a scene for *Melrose Place* where Heather was not on camera. In spite of the fact that she was sick and could have used a stand-in, Tracy says the actress delivered the lines to her costar. Be on the lookout for costars who are there for you even though no one else knows.

Be afraid. Be very afraid of costars who don't rejoice in your success. If they snipe at your blessings, minimize their scene time. And you certainly don't want to share scenes with cast mates who are forever telling you that you can't take on your intended role. It's one thing to say that it's tough to succeed in a particular field, quite another to say it's impossible. Associating with people who believe the latter is not going to help you. Look for costars who say, "Yes you can."

★ Keep sifting out of your life what Malawians call *umponga* friends. *Umponga* is an African word for rice, which is considered a delicacy in the place of my birth. In Malawi you don't want friends who only want to hang around when your plates are brimming with rice.

★ One of the best ways to widen your circle of costars is to entertain. Actor Steve Martin decided to widen his circle of friends by telling himself that he would have a certain number of dinner parties every month. You don't have to make several million dollars a picture in order to have folks over. Pasta costs pennies per serving.

★ If entertaining is too daunting, make it a point to go out a certain number of days a week, to art galleries, to street festivals, to political rallies (that support causes you believe in). Just get out there.

★ If you are finding it rough to find human costars consider adopting a furry friend.

Casting Breakdown

Casting directors and agents pay subscriptions for what are known as "casting breakdowns." They outline the acting roles available in upcoming productions. The list is detailed and includes specifics on such things as age range, body types, ethnic groups, and personality types. Here are some examples of actual breakdowns. One film called for a "Man 35–50, raincoat, briefcase, quiet observer of humanity in public places," and an independent film was in search of "Matt, quick, witty, subtle; Alex, tall, sarcastic, a bit cynical but not a jerk." Yet another production was extraordinarily demanding in its desires. Its listing said, "Actor must be proficient in the classics and prefer Shakespearean training. *Must be vegetarian!* [italics and exclamation point mine] . . . Male actor must have a knowledge of stage combat."

Diana Ross also looks for specific characteristics when casting for real-life musical costars when she goes on tour. She wants them to eat well. She'll pass on anyone who is into drug or alcohol abuse. And Diva Diana says anyone who goes on the road with her has to be punctual, and she wants her to take good care of herself. She says she quickly edits out gossips.

Make up your own requirements for the costars you want in your life. But first figure who is on the list now. Inventory the major players on the worksheet titled *Current Casting Breakdown*. Under *role description* list their characteristics, physical and mental.

Next create a list of your dream costars. Since you probably don't have names to list, simply describe the desired character and then list the desired characteristics on the *Starring Role Casting Breakdown* worksheet. Keep your descriptions reasonably brief. If you have trouble check back to my earlier examples.

As you fill out these forms you may see that you are already doing a really good job of casting. You might also see that you are missing something. Diversify. Look for more funny people. More artistic. More spiritual. If you really want to stretch, look for costars from a variety of backgrounds. They will introduce you to worlds that will help you add depth to your life script.

Current Casting Breakdown

Name:
Role description:

Name:
Role description:

Name:
Role description:

Name:
Role description:

Name:
Role description:

Starring Role Casting Breakdown

Name:
Role description:

Name:
Role description:

Name:
Role description:

Name:
Role description:

Name:
Role description:

Romantic Leads

Sharing your life stage with someone you love and who truly loves you can produce blinding radiance. That's why I tend to have serious questions about a relationship when I see either person losing his or her glow in the wake of a new romance. I've seen friends and acquaintances deteriorate after taking up with a new costar. They don't sleep enough, or they eat too much or too little or otherwise abuse themselves.

Singer Natalie Cole charted the negative medical effects of her romantic leading men. She says her blood pressure actually improved after going solo. Toxic relationships can be that destructive. Check your blood pressure. Look in the mirror and decide what effect your current romantic lead has on your star shine. Be honest. Has your romance enhanced or diminished it? Whatever consumes your romantic lead's life will surely end up taking over your life, too. That means you will be engulfed in drugs, violence, and bitterness if your intimate costar is. It's virtually impossible to avoid it.

Of course there is nothing more dazzling than to see a leading man and woman who really click. Think of Meg Ryan and Tom Hanks, Angela Bassett and Taye Diggs, Ruby Dee and Ossie Davis (of course their chemistry carried over into real life). That's what keeps many of us on the quest of casting the role of romantic lead by any means possible, even if it means submitting to everything from blind dates to dating services.

Open Auditions

A potential romantic lead will give you a lot of clues in the opening scenes. If he tells you he has trouble staying with one woman, believe him. Don't start a trousseau. If he tells you he needs his space, believe him. Open the door. If he says he doesn't want anything serious, believe him. Start laughing. Again I think of singer Natalie Cole who says that if a man acts like a jerk within the first twenty minutes of meeting him, odds are he is a jerk. The audition is over. Edit him out of your life the moment you see any early warning signals.

You know what kind of guy I am talking about. The kind who wants you to be a chorus girl when you are the star. I'm always a bit baffled by women who think they can revamp a romantic lead, whether it's his bad habits or sexual orientation. You've heard that saying that a man marries a woman hoping she will stay the same, and a woman marries a man in the hopes she can change him. It's a much better idea to start off with someone you want rather than to spend all of your life trying to do a rewrite.

Starring in your own life means sharing scenes with a romantic lead who supports your stellar role. Otherwise your closest of costars will be constantly trying to change you. And don't reject a leading man just because he's not tall enough, good-looking enough, or rich enough. Can you say "typecasting"? Sometimes the best costars are not the obvious choices. Reconsider what it is you really want and what you deserve.

Take stock of what your past romantic costars have had in common. I know when I made my list several years ago I noticed that I had several entries of people who were cold and distant. In those days I would beat my breast and ask myself, why do I end up with these men? Then I realized that the reason I was "ending up" with them was because I was purposely, if subconsciously, casting them. I did not want to get too close to anyone and the best way to insure that was to be with people who did not want to be close to me.

My actions back then were quite the opposite of *Diagnosis Murder* executive producer Chris Abbott, who told me how she made a star turn with her love life after a series of disappointing relationships. She boldly redirected the romantic scenes of her life script. She made it a rule to go out with several men at a time. Chris says she's monogamous by nature so going on multiple dates was a premeditated way of putting herself in a situation where she would not get intimate with anyone. When she realized that she was attracting men who were primarily attracted to her bank account, she decided to jettison some of the props that indicated wealth. She got rid of her flashy, expensive car and replaced it with solid but dependable wheels. Not too long after Chris made changes in her love scenes she met a solid dependable man. Today they are happily married.

★ When Julia Roberts was asked about her relationship with a man in her life, an interviewer compared his Hollywood star power with hers. Her response: "We are not what we do." Do not cast your costars just because of what they do. Believe me, bank account size does not equal generosity.

★ Pay attention to your romantic lead's motivations. The more time you two spend together the more important his motivations will become. They will guide your lives together. If his main motivation is to make money, don't be surprised if he spends most of his hours at the office.

★ If you are in search of a particular type of costar, you should go where that type of person would flock. It should be no mystery that I met a millionaire friend while traveling through Palm Beach, reportedly home to 1,700 millionaires. I met a successful musician when I was shooting a story at a New York nightclub. Mind you, I wasn't even looking. Imagine your success if you are actually scoping locations for possible costars.

★ Businesswoman Georgette Mosbacher makes no bones about having purposefully reached for the platinum ring on her way up when it came to enlarging her social circle. She did everything from hanging out at the fabled Polo Lounge to visiting auctions. At one such auction she met her first millionaire husband. Two more would be in her future, including former commerce secretary Robert Mosbacher.

★ If you don't know where to begin looking for a romantic
lead begin with your interests. Then investigate related
organizations. You want to be around other art lovers? The
obvious is joining an art museum. You can also check out
events at auction houses. Get on the mailing lists of galleries.
Sometimes that is no more difficult than calling or visiting
a gallery and saying that you want to be notified of their
openings. When you are on location visit area art houses.
Then start casting.

★ My literary agent, Jenny Bent, has a rule about romantic
leads. She believes you should go out with anyone who asks
you, at least once. Jenny says off the bat you have one thing in
common. You both like you.

★ Let your costars and supporting players know that you are
casting. They might help provide you with more candidates
to audition.

★ You are not going to meet anyone by sitting on the sofa
channel surfing. Go out there and find your own real-life
Denzel Washington or Hugh Grant instead of watching
romantic comedies on the tube.

★ After giving all these suggestions I will also add that my
mother's advice for finding romantic leading men is "unseek
and ye shall find." She means just go about living your life,
doing things you enjoy, and things will work out.

★ Although I was never a contestant on *Who Wants to Marry a
Millionaire?* at one time or another I have dated three or four
of them. Maybe five or six, but who is counting? I met all of
them while going about the business of living out my life
script. That's also how I met romantic leads rich in other
qualities, such as kindness and caring.

★ If you are bent on hooking up with a well-known star consider what happens when things are not going so well. I have found it becomes so much harder to get away from that person. There they are when you flip through a magazine or turn on the radio or television. This is also true if you get involved with a city councilman or business titan in your town. You can't get away from a well-known ex, even if your heart wants to.

★ Dialogue that never works for any romantic scene: "Without you I am nothing." "I'm available 24/7 so it's fine if you always call me at the last minute." "I'll destroy myself if you are not in my life." I write this as I'm watching a television biography about a beautiful television star who recited similar dialogue and attempted suicide a couple of times over failed romances until she finally succeeded. The lines don't work because when you star in your own life, you never forget how valuable you are. And most certainly you do not exist in the reflection of someone else's eyes.

★ Hollywood agents keep their clients under wraps to make them more desirable. One of the covenants of the book *The Rules* is that women should not be too available to their romantic lead. I don't believe in *playing* hard to get but I support *being* hard to get. Be so engaged in your starring role that romantic leading men feel privileged to share scenes with you. They are.

★ We don't even need to discuss how distasteful the whole Lewinskygate affair was, but it did tell me something about any man who says he is too busy to call. If the former leader of the free world had enough time to call Monica more than fifty times, can you honestly tell me that your romantic lead cannot spare a few minutes to call you? I know it's a tacky example but think about it the next time that hot clerk at Wal-Mart tells you he's too busy to call.

★ If you still want to make excuses for why he hasn't called, consider actor Frank Langella's observations about Hollywood. He says if producers want you, you could be in a remote desert and they'll slip a note under your tent. That's if they want you. So don't make excuses that your telephone was off the hook, or that your cellular phone must have been out of range. If he wants you he'll track you down.

Romantic Scenes

★ This may seem really cheesy, but look at the love scenes in soap operas. The soundtrack is sultry music. The set is filled with romantic props—candles and rose petals. Why can't you try it at home?

★ Spend a lazy Sunday viewing movies that exemplify the best of relationships, films that emphasize qualities such as equality, respect, and love. Then repeat those scenes in your real life.

★ For those days you are wondering why you cast your romantic leading man in the first place, rewind your wedding video. Relive the feelings that prompted you to walk down the aisle, the feelings that made you glow.

★ As I have been researching this book it's been amazing to read about the number of Hollywood stars who say they were physically abused. I'd heard about Pamela Anderson and Tina Turner in the news. But it was a surprise to read that men in the lives of Doris Day, Betty Grable, Ava Gardner, and Lana Turner beat them as well. It really can happen to anyone. If it's happening to you please get help. Just think of the post-Ike triumphs of the terrific Tina Turner.

Supporting Players

In the movies supporting players are there to help the main star shine more brightly, by providing everything from sympathetic banter to comedic relief. So it's no wonder they are called *supporting players*. While they may not have as many lines in your life as your costars, they do make a big difference in all of the scenes of your life. Nurture them. It will make going to the shoe repair shop, the dry cleaners, and the drugstore so much more pleasant if you have good rapport with the people who work there. They can be there for you in unexpected ways. Agent Pat Quinn told me she struggled through her first year at a major but unsupportive talent agency. She got the most positive human contact during her regular trips to the dry cleaner.

Supporting players have come through for me many times, including one New Year's Eve. My crazy schedule had me flying from New York to Washington, D.C., where I was working at the time. After an hour break I was set to catch another flight to Palm Beach. I was midway between my office and home when I spotted a homeless man who was a regular in my neighborhood. We had always exchanged greetings on the street. Just weeks earlier he was about to be kicked out of an office Christmas party at a fancy restaurant, when I told the organizers he was with me. "I'll never forget that," he said, offering to watch my bags so I could complete my errands. Because of this helpful supporting player I managed to catch my flight and spend New Year's in Florida. Countless other times supporting players have plied me with freebies, discounts, and other perks, just because I acknowledged their starring ways.

Recognize Them

★ Hollywood screenwriter Sharon Y. Cobb says when she is getting to know a mogul one of the first things she does is find out the name of Mr. or Ms. Big's personal assistant. She realizes the administrative assistant is an important gate-keeper who has a lot of sway in determining who gets an audience with the big cheese.

★ You might think that you can mistreat the supporting players of the stars in your universe. But consider the way of a Hollywood publicist who tells me that if a reporter treats her poorly when trying to set up an interview, they can just forget about going any further. She uses their behavior to gauge how her client will be treated.

★ There can be other consequences that come with not being nice to supporting players. A soundman I worked with told me about going on the road with a superstar singing diva. She so irked the road crew that they came up with a plan for revenge. Knowing the performer's choreography they plotted it out so when the singer took a dip her nose would come within inches of a pile of carefully arranged excrement.

Cultivate Them

★ A veteran television star once went undercover as a bellman and found that in uniform he was invisible, even when he was assisting Hollywood stars he knew. You miss out on a lot that way. When you are traveling supporting players can give you an insider's guide to a community. If I want to know the real scoop about a story I am covering, the first person I will ask is a local cab driver. They often have better insights than the local journalist covering the story.

★ Encourage the best and brightest of your supporting players. When she goes out of her way be helpful, make sure you shine a spotlight on what she has done. Speak to her boss. Or when it's appropriate, write a letter.

★ This is not to say that you don't offer a tip. Don't be like the politicos some Washington cab drivers call "quarterbacks." That's because the men and women on the hill routinely tip twenty-five cents, which means the driver gets only a "quarter back."

★ Keep lists of your most valuable supporting players. The shoe repairman, the manicurist, the taxicab driver. When I'm in Washington, D.C., I try to get Brooks to give me a ride because he always regales me with tales from his native Jamaica. His pleasant personality always makes the opening or closing act of my journey much more enjoyable.

Extras

They may have five lines or less in your life, but they contribute to the ambience. In fact they are called atmosphere in some circles. Of course, I am talking about extras. They are those people in the background who don't say much, if anything at all. They are your fellow passengers on the train, the people behind you at the check-out line, the drivers in your rearview mirror on the freeway. Their "screen time" in your life is fleeting. That doesn't mean that you can't use those moments as opportunities to bring light into your life, not to mention theirs. If you doubt the power of extras, think about the times when one has ruined your day. Just how upset were you when someone cut you off on the freeway or at the movies? Reverse roles. Consider how much better you will feel if someone lets you into the lane you need for your turn-off, or if you take care to let someone go ahead of you in line. It could end up being the brightest moment of your day.

An extra on a plane provided powerful radiance during some

recent dark days. My mother and I were returning from a trip to the east after a family tragedy. On top of everything our flights were canceled and then delayed because of snow. From the moment we boarded the first leg of our journey I noticed how one of the attendants appeared to be especially caring to all of the passengers. After our meal service I spoke with her for a moment about the circumstances of our trip. She was especially concerned about my mother arriving back in California so very late. We landed and ran to our connecting flight, which was already boarding. Moments later I was surprised to see our flight attendant standing at the gate, talking to the ticket agent. A few minutes later the agent told us that we had been upgraded to first class because of her. This dear flight attendant went as far as taking my mother's carry-ons to the plane. I almost cried. I could not believe that a stranger would go so far when in some instances it's hard to get a second glass of water from your flight attendant. This "extra" totally transformed what could have been a miserable day. Both my mother and I decided that night we wanted the flight attendant to have a long-running role in our lives.

Elevating an extra to a bigger role has happened before. I'll share an example that also involves travel. I was set to do an exclusive interview with the mother of the rapper Notorious B.I.G. and his sidekick Lil' Cease. But when I arrived at my Manhattan hotel there was no room at the inn in spite of confirmed reservations.

I was not happy. These were really important interviews and I wanted to be well rested for the early morning call time. From the hotel lobby I began calling other hotels and they, too, were full, which is amazing considering how many rooms there are in New York City.

There was another woman at the counter who had also been turned away. A national talk show, where she was set to appear the next day, had made her reservation. The show quickly made new arrangements. She saw my struggle. This stranger then offered that there were two double beds in the hotel room where she was headed. She said I could have one.

We were strangers then, but we have stayed in contact ever since. She is a magazine publisher and columnist who wrote an article about my mother a couple of years ago. As I write this we just exchanged messages via e-mail where she talked about another network appearance, and I gave her an update on my life. She's an extra who turned into a wonderful costar.

★ If you see someone on a busy street who looks lost, stop and show him the way. Of course always keep your safety in mind. When I do this it's just role reversal and a reminder of all the times people have stopped to help me.

★ When the person ahead of you doesn't know how to work the newfangled automated ticketing system, offer to show him how it works.

★ When a homeless person on the street asks for money, offer to get her food. Contribute through a shelter or your place of worship if you sense you are at all at risk.

★ Get up and offer your seat to the pregnant woman, the elderly man, the mother whose hands are full.

★ Smile at that office worker who looks as though she's had a rough day.

★ If you see someone dropping money, be sure to tell her. It could be the money she is counting on to pay the rent or for her next meal.

★ Warn the person who enters the bathroom stall after you that the toilet paper and seat covers have run out. For that matter, give a heads-up to the person who comes out of the bathroom stall with toilet paper streaming out of her panty hose.

★ Take care to park so your car door will not nick the paint on the car that is next to you.

★ Give room to the person signaling on the freeway ahead of you so he can exit onto the proper off-ramp.

★ Assist that fellow train or plane passenger with her luggage.

★ The grocery clerk, the guy behind the counter at the mini mart, the parking attendant may all feel like cogs in the machine. When dealing with them make a comment, no matter how brief, so that they know you realize that they are stars, too.

Fans

It's my favorite scene in the movie *Soapdish*. Sally Field, who plays a beleaguered soap opera actress, is having a rough day. Whoopi Goldberg, featured in the role of Sally's assistant, immediately knows what's next in the life script of her boss. Sally needs a fix. So she and Whoopi head to a familiar destination. Not to a bar or drug dealer. They actually end up at a nearby mall where Goldberg whips up the crowd, pointing and screaming at the boss she sees every day. "I watch you all the time!" "I can't believe I'm really meeting you!" As planned, her theatrics draw a crowd and soon Sally is surrounded by a group of admirers. Suddenly this soap star is shining again, thanks to the power of her fans.

Actress Nichelle Nichols changed her life after listening to a fan, albeit an especially impressive one. When mailroom employees confidentially told the *Star Trek* star that they had been instructed to hide her fan mail, Nichelle was so upset (understandably so) that she wanted to leave the show. But before her final day she went to a fund-raiser for the NAACP. There she was invited to meet a big fan, none other than civil rights leader Dr. Martin Luther King, Jr. When she informed him of her plans to leave the show, he implored her to change her mind. Dr. King told Nichelle that with her role as Lt. Uhura she had gone where roles for actresses of color had not gone before. So she stayed and went on to inspire everyone from Whoopi Goldberg to astronaut Dr. Mae Jemison.

The dictionary defines a fan as an enthusiastic follower or admirer. A supportive word from fans after a rough day has always renewed my sense of purpose. There have been times in the past that fans have often helped me keep going by believing in me when I was on an uncertain path. Are you glowing from your fans? While I want to offer tips on building your very own fan base, you have to begin by being a fan of yourself. Actress Katharine Hepburn once said, "I've always had a deep conviction of my charms." When you have that conviction you believe that you deserve the best of everything.

Be Your Own Fan

★ Appreciate your charms. Now is not the time to be modest. What are the things that you know you do well? Keep them foremost in your mind. Edit negative thoughts.

★ Also keep sentences such as "I'm not very good," "I'm not very smart," "I'm not very attractive" out of your dialogue.

★ Just like fan clubs do, keep track of what you do well. Revel in your awards, accomplishments, and compliments.

★ One way to do that is to keep reading this book. It's designed to make you recognize the best in you.

Building a Fan Base

★ Is there a place for you that is equivalent to Sally Field's shopping mall? A spot where you can go to be cherished, adored, and accepted? It could be an art gallery where your knowledge of black velvet Elvis art is esteemed, or the cooking class where your gingerbread men are so lifelike that they seem to walk off the cookie sheet. Collect frequent flyer miles going to places where you are admired.

★ Identify the easiest ways you can be in touch with your fans. It could be as simple as picking up the phone and calling your mother. Or maybe it's clicking on the Internet and connecting with your favorite uncle for an online chat.

★ I have always been impressed by the way former Chargers placekicker and onetime *Wheel of Fortune* host Rolf Bernischke would treat his fans. When folks would come up to him at functions, I would often eavesdrop. Instead of just listening when people would come to praise him, he immediately started asking questions about their lives. Try the same thing the next time a fan of yours approaches you. They will go away even bigger fans of yours.

★ Pay special attention to the terms of endearment you receive from children. Their praise is pure. One of my favorite compliments ever came backstage from children who had just come off the runway of a Givenchy fashion show in Paris, no less. In faltering English they told me they thought I was kinda cute. Their words meant more than if I had heard them from Denzel or Brad.

★ Television producer Aaron Spelling, who has scored phenomenal success with such television show hits as *Charlie's Angels*, *The Love Boat*, and *Melrose Place*, still takes time to listen to his fans. In fact when tour buses make treks to his über mansion, he says he actually comes out and polls fans to get feedback on his shows.

In Praise of Others

★ As a child I wrote a fan letter to popular comedian Flip Wilson. At the time he was the star of a top-rated variety show. Cut to a Sunday morning at brunch with my family. And who would knock on the door? Flip Wilson! Just because of my letter he drove all the way to San Diego from Los Angeles in his blue Rolls Royce, at the height of his fame. He then invited my family and me to see the taping of his show. I never dreamed my fan letter would take me so far. What a wonderful man. You never know where fan appreciation will take you.

★ Start a fan club. The first step in getting people to appreciate you is to appreciate others. If your child's teacher makes learning fun, send her a note. Or better yet notify the principal. You will all sparkle. I had a terrific boost after conducting a radio interview with broadcast legend the late Steve Allen. He went back to Los Angeles and wrote a fan letter telling a Los Angeles television station news director to hire me. The news director didn't, but Steve's support increased my resolve to go for a career in television.

★ Be the president of your child's fan club. I was at a television studio in Washington, D.C., where singer Brandy was performing. There was no audience except crew and family members. I scoped out the crowd of less than a dozen to try to figure out the identity of Brandy's father. You know how I was able to recognize him? No one was beaming brighter than he was as he watched yet another performance by his popular daughter.

★ If you are going to be a fan, be a fan. Don't be a critic with an identity crisis. You know, the kind of person who says, "You look great in those pants, they really disguise how big your bottom is." Edit after "You look good in those pants."

Villains

We like to boo and hiss villains but perhaps we should really be applauding them. Because if you interpret their character in the right way, they can inspire us more than any fans, costars, or supporting players. When a villain makes our professional or personal lives difficult, it forces us to reexamine what we are doing in life. Rough sailing makes us wonder why we are on the boat in the first place.

It's taken me a while to come to an understanding of how valuable villains can be. Think of Adam Sandler's football-playing character in the movie *The Waterboy*. Steroids don't power him. His strength comes from imagining his sports opponents are various villains.

Instead of being powered by put-downs, I used to suffer through them, destroying myself in little ways because of them, losing confidence because of what they said. I realize now that these miserable moments persisted because of a very willing costar—me.

Ultimately you are the one who gives power to villains. Perhaps they control or affect some aspect of your life. But they can't control *every* part. If you think so perhaps you have taken on the role of the victim. Take time to figure out the positive things you can do outside of the realm of your villains.

These days I do my best to look for ways of turning things around so villains ultimately bring light into my life. For example, this book would have been written at a slower clip were it not for a certain villain. Her every spiteful move prompted me forward.

Whenever I had an unpleasant encounter with this villain before lunch, I made sure that I used my meal break to write or mail twice as much as I originally planned. I never tried to sabotage this villain, although I knew that she would neglect to give me messages related to work events and social invitations. The trick was not allowing myself one moment to wallow in her unkindness.

Screenwriter Sharon Y. Cobb, who has written a film that Danny Glover is signed on to star in, has also harnessed the power of villains to take her to the next level. Sharon had been putting off making her move to Hollywood. In the meantime she was working as an executive for a magazine publication in Florida. A villain at the company was so unkind that it prompted her to move to Los Angeles and pursue her dream on an accelerated schedule.

Sharon has an effective way of depersonalizing villainy. She tells me that when she meets one she immediately opens up an imaginary book titled "things a jackass says." Instead of taking offense at what the villain says, Sharon enters their conversations into the book. When she no longer has to deal with that person she closes the book and throws it away.

There are multiple Bible verses where God says he will take care of everything in the vengeance department. I don't think I have ever seen a villain get off without getting what they deserved and then some. It's a waste to spend your time hating and plotting against them, or envying their seeming success. Remember what I said about using your energies to tend to your own garden. Plus you'll end up with a beautiful garden that way.

Limit Their Moments in Your Spotlight

★ I don't care how exclusive the restaurant is or how trendy the clothing shop, why would you want to stuff the pockets of someone who doesn't care for you? You may have heard Groucho Marx say that he wouldn't want to belong to any club that would have him as a member. Perhaps it's that mentality that will make you patronize a business where the villainous supporting players do not treat you with respect. These villains are so easy to cut out of your life. Simply start to go to businesses that treat you with respect.

★ There are periods in almost all of our lives when we have to share some scenes with villains. It can be particularly tough if the villain is your boss. I developed one way of dealing with a verbally abusive honcho. When I knew I was scheduled to meet with him to be berated, I would write down a list of all my good qualities and read them over and over again before meeting with him. It severely lessened the impact of these encounters.

★ You might feel obliged to be around villains at work, but see what you can do about minimizing them in your personal life. Remember the laundry analogy? The villains will start to rub off on you.

If you believe that villains are a roadblock to your path, sit down and draw an escape plan. Illustrate your starting point and your destination. Methodically plot out exactly how your villain is keeping you from your dream. I'll bet you that in black and white the villain seems much less powerful. As you are plotting, think detour. Never let a villain keep you from where you want to go because then they win.

★

Character Examination

This may sound kind of odd, but take time to figure out what's good about the villain. That's right—I said to look for the good.

There was one villain I worked with for many years who I thought was extremely artificial. He was always sweet to your face, but I would hear him talk trash about every single one of the people who were close to him. Of course I too was vivisected by his sharp tongue. Sources told me he constantly made derogatory comments on everything from my appearance to my intelligence.

This chatty villain would want to tell me everything about the people in his circle from their drinking habits to their sex lives. I was bewildered to be the recipient of these confidences since I was never this guy's friend. So what was good about him? You would have to go far to find someone who bought as many gifts, little ones mind you, for his supporting players. For some of them it was their only recognition. While the back stabbing of his colleagues was reprehensible, remembering his supporting players was commendable. Is there something that you can learn from your villains?

★ Try to figure out what motivates the villains in your life: an unhappy childhood, an unsuccessful love life. It's no excuse for their behavior but at least if you understand what is behind their actions it takes away some of the sting.

★ No matter how angry a villain makes you, responding with physical violence is just not an option. Think about those stories in the news when someone strikes out at a villain. Everyone close to that person is also hurt.

★ If your villain was a former romantic leading man, it's all the more important that you don't center your life on revenge. Becoming consumed by revenge is MAD—Mutually Assured Destruction. Want proof? Rent the dark comedy *The War of the Roses*. Not to mention that wrath can wreak havoc on your health. A study at the University of North

Carolina at Chapel Hill found that if you are prone to anger you are nearly three times more likely to have a heart attack.

Grow from It

★ Make sure you don't become the victim of role reversal. That's where you take on the very characteristics that you don't like about the villains in your life. Just because you're the one spewing the dialogue doesn't make the role any more inviting.

★ Before doing anything negative, I try to remember that any negative actions will simply make the villain happy. On more than one occasion that thought has stopped me from doing something self-destructive.

★ As hard as it may be, on occasion listen to those who are against you. That's what Madonna does. When she and her colleagues were doing a research screening for the movie *Truth or Dare* they actually solicited people who said they hated Madonna. They put out a better movie that way. Put out a better life that way.

★ Historically my way of dealing with villains has been to edit, to simply cut them out of my life to whatever degree is possible. The ultimate way of dealing with your villain, of course, is something that is still a challenge to me. The Bible tells us to turn the other cheek. I would rather just turn and run. It's something I really have to work on. What about you?

Don't waste a moment to begin casting for your life. Go ahead and invite that bilingual librarian to lunch. See if your daughter's feisty basketball coach would like to go to a WNBA game with you. Go shopping with your artistic new neighbor. Do it now.

If you cast correctly expect your health to improve. And I'm not just talking about lowering your blood pressure. A Harvard study found that socializing added an average of two years to the lives of senior citizens, an impact that is comparable to the effect of exercising (though this is no excuse for you to substitute a pizza date for pumping iron). Researchers also believe that friends improve your immune system, reduce depression, and increase memory. And get this: Folks with fewer friends tend to have more accidents.

Part of it may be that you are healthier. Being surrounded by the best of friends makes you feel good on the inside, but your starring role does not stop there. The next step is to do some work on the outside.

When I am a star I will be every inch
and every moment a star.
— ACTRESS GLORIA SWANSON

★

CHAPTER EIGHT

Get Ready for Your Close-up

Makeup, Personal Training, and Wardrobe

The mega diva arrived at the studio with a mega entourage that included her own lighting person, a makeup person, and someone whose job, it seemed, was to pull down the mega diva's skirt. She also came equipped with astounding physical beauty. But the show's producer noted and later told me there was no glow from the inside. It goes to show you that you can't fake the glow. You can enhance it though, by dressing up, working out, and making up—your attitude.

Look the Part

True stars are easy to recognize, with or without an entourage. They sparkle with radiance that even the most skilled makeup artist could never imitate. After working with dozens of makeup people myself, I've come to recognize that although pigment and paint can help, the best beauty aid is not found in a bottle. You don't have to trek to the dermatologist or plastic surgeon. Your wallet doesn't have to be loaded with hundred-dollar bills to buy the latest beauty cream. A smile will enhance your mouth more than any lipstick. A twinkle in your eye is more beguiling than any eyeshadow. Serenity will smooth the surface of your skin better than any super-exfoliating, alpha-hydroxy-retinoic cream.

I haven't always been a student of the "beauty from the inside" school. I used to think, "Point me in the direction of the M·A·C makeup counter and leave me alone." But I became a believer a few years ago when on assignment in San Jose, California.

I was to do an interview with a grieving mother who had just lost her son. She was a hardworking woman of limited means. I wanted the shot of her to highlight the sincere and feminine woman she was. No harsh lights. Plus I wanted a soft backdrop. The cameraman did not seem to get it and that just made me more frustrated. In the middle of creating this particular mise-en-scène my soundman asked, "How old are you?" for no particular reason. "Well, what do you think?" I asked, more than slightly annoyed. "Well, when I first saw you I would have guessed a younger age," he said thoughtfully. "But now I'm not so sure."

Talk about stress making you old. Here I was aging right before this technician's very eyes. That's why I say that getting ready for your close-up doesn't begin with your foundation or skin care. It starts much deeper than that. Haven't you known someone who does not have classically beautiful features but is still regarded as beautiful? If you were to put her next to someone with those classic features but who is radiance-challenged, she would come across as the more fetching of the two. It's because she has mastered the biggest beauty secret of them all: star shine.

★ Don't beat yourself up for not looking like that gorgeous woman you saw in a magazine. That woman probably doesn't look like that either. I was appalled when I saw a documentary that featured the behind-the-scenes of a leading women's magazine. It showed editors planning to airbrush the wrinkles from the face of a seventeen-year-old! Yes, I said a seventeen-year-old. That's how unrealistic the images that surround us can be. So don't pay attention.

★ Don't flip through magazines wishing that you were younger, blonder, or slimmer. Some arbiters of style would like us to believe that there is only one way to be beautiful. But just look at the variety of stars in the heavens. There is just as much variety in the constellation of stars in Hollywood, where through my telescope Whoopi Goldberg sparkles as brightly as Julia Roberts. Look for media outlets that celebrate your kind of beauty. That way you'll also be getting tips on enhancing your brand of beauty from pros.

★ Maybe you are complaining, "I have too many wrinkles." Ava Gardner had the right attitude when she said, "Whatever wrinkles are there I've enjoyed getting them." While you are at it, edit the following dialogue: "Boy my pores are too big." "I wish I had skin like Angela Basset." "If only my nose were smaller." Instead, pick up a few jars of mental makeup. Apply liberally. Instead of complaining silently as you apply your makeup that you were not born with Naomi Campbell or Cindy Crawford's features, keep repeating to yourself how wonderful yours are. Then start truly believing it. The number of compliments you get after applying this mental makeup may surprise you. Legendary film star Sophia Loren lists "good thoughts" as one of her essential beauty secrets.

When designer Diane Von Furstenberg sees herself in the
mirror she says, "Hi, Sweetie."

★ Your internal dialogue impacts your external appearance.
During a shoot a photographer told model-actress Isabella
Rossellini that he did not like what she was thinking. Mind
you, he did not know what she was thinking. He could see it
in her eyes! Before the shoot ended Isabella says she wanted
to test the photographer, so she went back to her original
thought. Well, he caught on right away and told her "I told
you, I don't like that. Change it." What thoughts can others
see on your face?

★ Value yourself. It's harder for others to think that you are terrific if you yourself don't think so. I said a variation of this earlier but it's worth repeating. Imagine if you went to a grocery
store and they were selling caviar for four dollars a tin rather
than four hundred. Selling yourself short takes away from
your intrinsic beauty. That image will reflect in the mirror.

★ Confidence is a major beauty secret. When the late Brandon
Tartikoff was the head of NBC, hits such as *Miami Vice, Hill
Street Blues,* and *The Cosby Show* were on the prime-time
schedule. During the casting process Brandon said he
watched very closely how actors carried themselves in and
out of the room. Were they enthusiastic? Were they sponta-
neously funny? He found that star quality went far beyond
physical features. Actress Fran Drescher says her mother
taught her that no matter how much weight she might be carrying around, she should "sell it to the world as voluptuous,
with confidence and no apologies, and the world will respond
as such." Sell it, Sister.

★ At the beginning of her career Ingrid Bergman would go to
work with her then-husband. But he would drop her off be-

fore they got to the studio door. She then would ride her bike the rest of the way. Her former husband was not being mean. He just wanted her to arrive with a glow. Work out just before that important interview, meeting, or special appearance. It will siphon off some of the stress you may be feeling. Plus it will give you a healthy sparkle, better than any makeup.

★ Before that all-important meeting don't forget to pick up a dose of joy. Talk to a friend who makes you smile. Rent a comedy that makes you laugh. Read a few chapters of that book that always cracks you up. Think of it as a foundation to your foundation.

★ If you are hanging with folks who love olive-skinned babes with long hair and you happen to be chocolate-hued with close-cropped hair, there may be a problem. After a while you are likely to feel like less than zero. In that case, remember, there are fan clubs out there for virtually every type of woman, even if you are heavy, bald, or an amputee. There are magazines, organizations, and Web sites that celebrate all of the above. But beware of folks who like you just because of your unique characteristics.

Finding Your Look

When I was that awkward little girl intent on fighting for my starring role, I worked a lot to beautify my mind. But a torrent of ugly comments about my appearance made it clear I had to work on my exterior. People made judgments based on what they saw before they ever got a chance to know me. Later in life I would see this "lookist" viewpoint in play when I pitched potential interview subjects for television segments and had to deal with the question "Are they good-looking?" Mind you, the question was not "Are they well-spoken?" It makes you understand why we go so far to look better. You get a better sense of why actress Jodie Foster reportedly racked up a bill of twelve thousand dollars to cover her hair and makeup for her appearance on the news program *60 Minutes*. As much as I resent it sometimes my looks have had an effect on my starring role. I've been told that news moguls did not want to hire me for no other reason than they did not like my appearance. Of course those same features have won me jobs.

Even outside of Hollywood it can pay to know your way around a powder puff. A study of the wages of women ranging from low-paying jobs to Harvard MBAs found that salaries went up along with the ability to skillfully apply makeup.

Actress Ann Magnuson got a sense of the psychic cost of not looking good when she went undercover as an "ugly" person. Working with a makeup artist she came up with what she considered to be a loathsome look. It included crooked prosthetic teeth and clunky shoes. Magnuson says she was shunned everywhere during her excursion. People were so cold that at one location even the ". . . doorman refused to say what the store sold."

So the idea here is not to obsess about what you look like but to make judicious improvements to try to look your best.

★ As I mentioned earlier, the sneers and jeers I got as a child sent me scurrying to the library to find books to work on the outside as well as the inside. Books will always be a great resource, but there are many other places these days to go for guidance on putting together a star appearance. That includes videos, CD ROMs, and the Internet.

★ Are friends always telling you that you resemble a particular Hollywood star? Closely analyze that personality's appearances in newspapers, magazines, and television. In some cases there will even be a listing of the exact brand and color of makeup the star is wearing. You may say, "Those aren't my colors," or "I never wear makeup." But consider that a team of professional beauty experts is guiding this star. Learn something. Plus it's one beauty consultation that won't cost you a dime.

★ When you are cruising the makeup counter aisles, don't just stop at the one that sells your favorite brand. Pay as much attention to the line's representative. How does her appearance fit with your starring role? If the fishnets and aubergine highlights on the salesperson behind the counter match your own you will probably do better there than with the rep who looks like Grace Kelly.

★ When looking for beauty services, go to neighborhoods that match the look you are striving for. If you are in Los Angeles you are more likely to get a hairstylist expert in giving you a neon-blue Mohawk on Melrose Avenue than you are on Rodeo Drive. If your starring role is edgy, go to downtown New York. If you want to look more like a lady who lunches, go uptown.

★ Audition hairstyles by checking out one of those computer programs that allow you to virtually change your coiffure. Buy the program. Sample it on the Internet. Use it at a salon.

★ You might also try a 3-D dress rehearsal by going to a wig shop and trying various styles and colors. See which ones work best. Straight or curly? Full or sleek?

★ Don't wait to unveil your starring look—until you lose ten pounds, or until you get that raise, or until the kids are a bit older. Debut it now. Don't be a spectator. What are you waiting for?

★ If your "before" look is discouraging you might feel better after taking a look at the images of Hollywood stars before they made it big. A striking example is Greta Garbo. It's proof positive of how much you can benefit from expert assistance, be it a friend or a professional.

★ Don't fall into the "everyone else is doing it trap," especially if the results will be permanent. When my mother was growing up, everyone in her African village sported elaborate designs on their faces and bodies. The village beauty practitioner would make a series of cuts on the skin and then rub in charcoal to create raised scars. To this day my mother has those markings on her tummy, but she resisted getting them on her beautiful face, which made her all the more ready for her close-up when she came to America and appeared on television, in newspapers, and on magazine covers.

★ Think twice about making over the physical quirk that makes you unique. It's a virtue—not a vice—*not* to look like everyone else. What if model Lauren Hutton did not have a gap between her two front teeth? She was advised to disguise it. What if Cindy Crawford did not have that mole above her lip? In the beginning beauty "experts" told her to get rid of it.

★ Don't make any changes because of spite. You are breaking up with your romantic lead. He liked long hair, so you might decide to lop your locks off. You won't be getting even with him if you look better in Godiva-like tresses.

★ But changing your life may be the perfect time to change your appearance. Garbo did when she left films. Something as seemingly superficial helped set her on the road to a new life. A makeover could do the same for you as you change careers, settings, or your romantic lead.

★ Go through old photos and determine which style in the past has looked the most fetching on you. If your face still has the same contours, maybe that Dutch boy that made you glow as a child would still work today. Also review any home video-tape for ideas.

★ You may not be posing for a magazine cover, but fix yourself up for that driver's license and passport photo. You'll have to see your license almost every day. Why not make the most of it? As for your passport photo, there is no excuse to have a bad one because you get to choose it.

★ Find a star scent. Make it your signature. Amarige by Givenchy is mine. When I wear it I get more compliments than when I wear any other fragrance. So it's part of my un-seen uniform on special occasions. Collect department store perfume samples of your signature scent and keep them in your purse.

Personal Training

Actress Faye Dunaway reportedly lost thirty pounds for her star-making role in the movie *Bonnie and Clyde.* Actor Robert De Niro did just the opposite for the movie *Raging Bull.* He packed on an amazing sixty pounds when he took on the part of prizefighter Jake LaMotta. Both stars were willing to transform their bodies for parts, albeit good ones, that lasted fewer than ninety minutes onscreen. How far are you willing to go to get into shape for a role that lasts a lifetime?

Now, I am not suggesting that you wear sandweights around your wrists, ankles, and waist and eat nothing but eggs and grape-fruit, like Dunaway reportedly did. But there is no way of escap-ing that getting physical is part of the package. That's why you are as likely to see Hollywood stars at the gym as you are at a pre-miere.

You don't have to join a gym. You don't even have to work out every day. But find a way to write workouts into your life script. Haven't you seen how radiant healthy people are? When I think of the exercise mavens I've met or interviewed over the years, including Richard Simmons, Kathy Smith, and Jack and Elaine Lalanne, one thing they have in common is vibrancy.

My seat was just a few rows behind John F. Kennedy Jr. at former President Bill Clinton's first inaugural. I was not prepared to be taken with him. Before seeing him in the flesh, of course I had seen all of the media coverage. The sexiest man alive. Blah, blah, blah. Well, in person he positively radiated. Part of it was confidence. But what I also saw on that chilly day in January was someone who looked incredibly healthy. His vitality easily eclipsed the Hollywood stars that surrounded him, including his movie star date.

Mind you I have not always been a champion of exercise. One of my junior high school classmates reminded me of how we would hide behind the bleachers to avoid jogging around the track. Boy, how things have changed! These days my time at the gym is often my favorite part of the day (though I'm still not exactly what you would call a hard-core jock). A viewer once told me to my face that I ran "like a girl" after seeing me take part in an exhibition game at the San Diego Sports Arena with the famed Harlem Globetrotters. But no matter, I have found that exercise prompts me to glow from the inside and even sing.

One of the great things about exercise is that unlike other stress relievers (such as drugs and alcohol) you look and feel better afterward. Not to mention that the other unhealthy stuff wreaks havoc with your glow. If you need proof of this, look at the before/after photos of any aging, partying rock musician of your choice. I'm not trying to be mean, but just track their appearance over a ten- or twenty-year period. Ask yourself: Do I really want to go through those changes? On the other hand, try tracking the appearance of the physically fit over the same amount of time. Proof of this came when I was watching a television segment that showed identical twins. One smoked. The other did not. The former drank alcohol. The latter did not. Guess which one looked younger?

Working out can change the heavy drama of your life into a light comedy. Studies show that exercise elevates your moods as it boosts serotonin and endorphin levels. It's all at your fingertips. Would we not all be in line to sign up for a magical cure that promised to reduce the incidence of everything from stress to cancer to heart disease, stroke, and even Alzheimer's? The fact that physical activity also improves the outer you almost becomes secondary.

Pre-production

It annoys me when spectators dismiss the fabulous shape of some Hollywood star by saying, "It's easy for _____ to keep in shape because she has all that money to afford the best trainer." Whether you are a princess or a pauper, it requires discipline to keep fit. All the money in the world doesn't matter if you don't have the will to take care of yourself. The trick is to come up with a regimen that matches your character.

Remember going through the pre-production process earlier? I suggest that you go into the same mode as you figure out how to develop your body of work. Begin by researching what works best for you. And please don't lace up a Nike, don a leotard, or snap on a sports bra without first checking with your doctor.

★ Ask your doctor what she thinks you need to work on. Strength? Endurance? Fat burning?

★ After that conversation go to the library. Go to dot-com land. Browse through magazines at the checkout counter. See what fitness-forward cities such as Los Angeles are up to. Frequent visits and then a move back to California have given me a chance to see lots of fitness trends before they spread to the rest of the country and the world.

Act III

Develop an image of what you will look like once you have achieved your fitness goals. As a visual aid find a magazine photo that resembles where you want to go. But be realistic. If you are round, look for someone who is also round—but in good shape. If you are petite, look for someone who reflects your stature.

An entertainment magazine got into trouble when it put Oprah's head on Ann-Margret's body for a cover. But it's okay for you to paste your head onto your dream body. Some computer graphic programs will help you create an even more realistic-looking piece of art. Or maybe you have a ready-made photo of yourself during a healthier time. When you get your artwork together paste it onto the *Personal Training Act III* Worksheet. Get specific and write down how much you want to weigh. What exact measurements make sense for you? Attach a date to when you will achieve this fit status. Again, talk with your doctor about your goals.

★ Make copies of your creation and then put it on strategic display in your home gym, in your office desk drawer, on your fridge, near the couch you inhabit when you are scheduled to work out. Or keep a copy in your wallet.

★ Champion Andre Agassi wins his tennis matches in his mind before ever picking up a racket. Start visualizing how you will feel with a winning, healthy body. Imagine how much easier it will be to climb the stairs. To walk to the dry cleaners. To negotiate your way through the airport.

★ ★ ★ ★ ★ ★ ★ ★ ★ ★ ★ ★ ★ ★ ★ ★ ★

Personal Training Act III
My Star Look

To be achieved by (date) _____

★ ★ ★ ★ ★ ★ ★ ★ ★ ★ ★ ★ ★ ★ ★ ★ ★

Act I

Make a record of your current state. How far can you go the distance on the treadmill? What level is comfortable for you on stationary bikes? How much weight can you lift? How flexible are you right now? Your doctor should be able to provide more information such as your blood pressure and cholesterol readings. On the worksheet labeled *Personal Training Act I* make a listing of your current measurements: bust, waist, and hips; arms, thighs, and legs. At the end of Act I record today's date.

★ ★ ★ ★ ★ ★ ★ ★ ★ ★ ★ ★ ★ ★ ★ ★ ★

Personal Training Act I

Bust_____

Waist_____

Hips_____

Thighs_____

Upper arms_____

Calves_____

Body fat percentage_____

Today's date_____

★ ★ ★ ★ ★ ★ ★ ★ ★ ★ ★ ★ ★ ★ ★ ★ ★

Act II

On the worksheet titled *Personal Training Act II* keep a log of what you will be doing every week in order to get to Act III. Then do your best to follow your script. Of course, don't beat yourself up when you miss a few days now and then. Every month or so see how well you are sticking to your script. Don't weigh yourself every day. Do it once a week so you don't get discouraged by daily fluctuations, such as water retention, that have nothing to do with your true weight. Hollywood stars often try on a particular pair of jeans to gauge how well they are doing instead of getting on a scale. Use one slightly snug outfit to help you keep track of your progress. Make "I am strong," "I am fit," and "I have muscles" part of your fitness program dialogue. Edit when you catch yourself saying, "I'm so fat," "I cannot stand this cellulite," or "I am so flabby."

Work in a workout whenever you are feeling weak and helpless. Then start feeling like one of those action-adventure heroines.

★ ★ ★ ★ ★ ★ ★ ★ ★ ★ ★ ★ ★ ★ ★ ★ ★

Personal Training Act II

Log of personal training for the week of _____

Log of personal training for the week of _____

Log of personal training for the week of _____

★ ★ ★ ★ ★ ★ ★ ★ ★ ★ ★ ★ ★ ★ ★ ★ ★

Finding a Gym

Audition gyms. All health clubs have a vibe. Look for one with qualities that will make it irresistible for you to stick with the program. The cheapest gym is not necessarily the best bargain, especially if you never go. You'll need all the incentives you can get because one study finds that half of all gym members stop going within three months.

Some gyms are designed for women. Some are more family-oriented and provide baby-sitting services. Some are very hip and trendy such as the gym where it seemed I couldn't go to a class without seeing a Hollywood star. At that club it made me chuckle when some members worked out in their sunglasses. I've been to gyms equipped with valets. At one such gym it seemed the patrons could have gotten their exercise by lifting their multicarat diamond-studded hands. When I was auditioning gyms I decided that the air at that particular club was too rich for me. I'm the type who likes to go in with little fanfare, work out, and leave. What makes you comfortable?

★ Try to visit the gym at least a couple of times during the period you will be doing most of your workouts. How does the parking stack up? Will you be able to get within ten feet of your favorite excercise machines? Do the instructors on the schedule inspire you?

★ If you enjoy regular changes in the scenery, find a gym that has more than one location. My current club has branches in many communities, each with a different flavor. There is a hip-hop class with a live deejay at my favorite location. The branch closest to my home has a much more conservative repertoire and client base. It's great to have a choice, because sometimes I feel like a nut; sometimes I don't.

★ Review the soundtrack played at the club. Will it move you? These days clubs are offering all kinds of music from the aforementioned live deejays and African drums to live gospel choirs.

★ Before you sign up for a gym it's a legitimate question to ask how the facilities are cleaned. At my club I am happy to say there has been someone from the housekeeping staff on duty during virtually every time I've visited.

★ Do you prefer to do most of your workouts alone? Then you may not want to join a club that offers lots of classes. The no-frills approach could save you money. Just make sure there is an adequate selection of free weights and machines.

★ So what, you don't have a personal trainer coming to your house. Just make sure to have a gym that's close to you. When I lived in Chevy Chase, Maryland, I could almost roll out of my bed into my health club. It was right next door. That was a major reason I selected it. If your club is out of the way it's just one more excuse not to go.

★ Your friend who belongs to a gym is likely to have free guest passes. Ask if you can tag along for a no-cost workout.

★ Are you going to feel uncomfortable if everyone is considerably slimmer than you are? One survey showed that as many as one-fourth of the women said self-consciousness was a barrier to working out. It's no excuse and don't let that stop you. There are gyms designed for fuller-figured exercisers. Go. If there is not one in your community, form your own group with similarly minded workout partners. I always look for a fair proportion of people who are in worse shape than I am in, so I won't be totally discouraged (a particular challenge when I am in South Beach, Florida). Then I also look for a percentage of my workout mates to be in better shape. They serve as inspiration.

★ If you want to take care of business at your gym, get recommendations from your professional colleagues. I recently heard a television executive talking about networking, not through her contacts from her alma mater, Harvard, but through her health club.

★ You can also cast for your personal life at the gym. Word is Jerry Seinfeld met Mrs. Seinfeld while working out. If you are in your twenties and most of the people at the club are in their fifties that may not be the place for you. Or perhaps if you are a professional and most of the other people in your club are college students, you may not be able to easily cast from that field of potential costars. Or then again it could be the perfect setting.

★ Keep in mind that if you cast a romantic lead from your health club, that romance could lose steam. Think about how you will feel about watching him pump up his heart after he has broken yours.

★ Don't join a gym that's open from seven in the morning to ten at night if you can't get there before 11 P.M. If you feel constricted by a club's schedule, look for one that is open twenty-four hours a day.

★ Get everything you can when you are first signing up at a gym. Do the physical assessment. See if they will throw in some free sessions with a personal trainer. Go for a free massage session. The gym will be most motivated to give it up when you are coming onboard.

★ Never join a club because you feel pressured to sign on the dotted line. It's unlikely that you'll ever feel really comfortable there. Don't fall for the line "You can only get this price if you sign up today." Call ahead. Get a feeling of what it will cost you before you go in person.

At the Gym

★ Once you have signed up at a gym, keep class schedules everywhere: on your fridge, in your office, in your car. That way you have no excuses when you decide to take a class at the last minute.

★ I drink a liter and a half of water during my spin classes. Instead of having to remember to bring a bottle to each class, I keep my supply in my car trunk. Your gym sells water, you say. It costs me about a quarter of the price to bring my own. Also supply your own fruit, muffins, or health bars unless you want to be lighter in the pocket.

★ If you arrive at an aerobics class late it's a definite no-no to stand in front of someone who has already taken a position. Health club regulars often have their star position in front of a mirror. Don't mess with it.

★ Multimillion-dollar stars such as Oprah and Cher have their own personal trainers. You can, too. Sort of. Look around for the buffest person in your circle. Ask to join them at the gym and go through the paces. I used to do this with über-buff TV cameraman Gary Buydos when I was in San Diego. The bonus was that he would also give me rides on his Harley. Arthur, who runs the Washington Versace store, has also served as my pretend personal trainer, offering loads of tips. Loren from the store also helped.

★ When you cast about for personal trainers, why not check into the P.E. Department at your neighborhood high school? Or query your favorite aerobics teacher to see if she is trained to be a personal trainer.

★ If you hire a personal trainer see if she will let you videotape your workout. That way you can replay it when she's not around or when you are on the road.

★ Share the cost of a personal trainer by sharing your session with a friend or two. It's best if you are all at similar fitness levels.

★ When you are working out on the treadmill, don't bring along that business report that is due next week. Researchers say that when they compared college women on a bike who studied and those who didn't, the group that worked out without the books felt better afterward.

On Your Own

★ If you cannot find the right gym remember your body won't know if you are at home in your den or at a club. Start off working out with a video or friend.

★ Your workout doesn't have to be a massive makeover. Researchers at the Cooper Institute of America found that something as simple as taking the stairs or walking to lunch rather than driving will give you the same results as your more traditional workout.

★ If you are thinking about equipping yourself with a home gym, do it gradually. Don't immediately bring home that $5,000 super-duper treadmill. Instead, buy some weights and tubing to gauge how well you work out on your own.

★ See if any of your friends or acquaintances are using their rowing machines or stationary bikes as clothing valets. You may be able to get a good deal on used equipment that way.

★ Plus there are plenty of exercises that do not require any equipment. Can you say push-up? Sit-up?

★ Look to your cupboards and refrigerator for cheap workout weights. You can pump water bottles and tin cans.

★ Dress up your set for your workouts. Do as I've seen them do at my gym during yoga and belly dancing classes. Light a candle. Just be sure to place it in a safe place.

Workout Wear

★ Your wardrobe, especially your shoes, can go a long way toward enhancing your workout. I was spinning for at least a year before I bought the spin shoes. I don't know why I waited so long. What a difference in my workout! The same can apply to shoes for aerobics, walking, and running.

★ Under it all wear a hardworking sports bra, something that's especially important if you are top-heavy. These bras come in a variety of styles these days. Don't leave home for the gym without one.

★ Make sure you look the part of a physically active person. Have at least a couple of gym-worthy outfits that compliment your coloring and figure. Do not wear white tights unless you really want to add apparent inches to your thighs. Matte, dark, Lycra-rich leotards may not be able to get rid of cellulite but they can go a long way to smooth out your legs.

★ A trick popular on the set of *Baywatch* was to diminish the appearance of cellulite with a tan. Now, you know I can't recommend getting one from the sun, but why not get one from a bottle? Plus don't forget that old-fashioned muscles can also be an effective antidote to the appearance of cellulite.

★ Wear your personal training "wardrobe" as often as possible. For example, when you come home, before fixing dinner put on your workout wear. You will be more likely to go to the gym or walk around the block if you are already suited up.

★ Keep your gym clothes packed up in your car and make them the first thing you put into your suitcase. That way you can't use the excuse "I don't have a thing to wear."

Variety Show

Madonna says the key to her workout success is consistency and variety. She never does the same thing twice a week. At least once try the latest exercise fad you keep hearing about (after checking with your doctor, of course). I always hear the experts talking about the importance of cross training for a well-rounded workout, not to mention body.

Variety sure makes working out seem like less drudgery. Exploring options led me to my favorite exercise of all: spinning. I've also tried African dance, step, funk, ballet, tap, kickboxing, yoga, and even belly dancing. But I keep my eyes open for something I might even like better.

★ An increasing trend for Hollywood stars is to work out in ways that are good for the soul as well as the body. Put more laid-back classes into your schedule such as yoga, stretching, or Pilates.

★ If you feel as though you are getting into a rut, get a one-day pass to the best gym in your city. Schedule it on a day when you can take full advantage of the health club's schedule. It shouldn't cost more than twenty dollars. Consider it the healthful equivalent of chocolate-covered bonbons.

★ Do not confine your workouts to the gym. Regularly change locations: the park, the town square, a beautiful garden.

Lena Nozizwe

★ Or try the shopping center. Use your love for shopping to get you to the mall. Once you get there do some power walking. As you briskly pass the windows, admire the clothing and think about how much better it will look on your increasingly fit body. Check to see if your shopping center offers organized walks.

★ Wherever you go keep safety in mind. Traditionally I have been a big fan of taking the stairs instead of the elevator, especially when going to the gym. (The sight of elevator riders working out on the StairMaster always befuddled me.) That is until I talked to folks in law enforcement who say that stairwells are not always safe. Losing extra calories is not worth risking your well-being.

★ Another note on safety: Don't pump up the volume on your portable stereo during your outdoor workouts. It's easy to lose yourself in the groove. Then you don't notice criminals moving in for an attack.

Wardrobe

I'll never forget the first words I heard out of the mouth of Oscar-nominated actress Elizabeth Shue. The location was the opening of a Las Vegas club. The paparazzi and television crews from *Entertainment Tonight* and *Access Hollywood* lined the red carpet. My microphone was poised, but before I had a chance to ask my question, Elizabeth had one of her own. "Vivienne Tam?" I replied, "Yes," in a lilting voice that could not disguise more than a modicum of pride that she had recognized my sale frock that was indeed made by Viv. So even before my first question we were conversing in the Hollywood language of fashion.

You may not recall any specific dialogue from the movies *Flash-*

dance, *Saturday Night Fever,* or *Annie Hall,* but you remember the ripped, off-the-shoulder T-shirts, the white three-piece suit with the black shirt, and Annie's mannish vest and tie. Even the down-home author Mark Twain said, "Clothes make the man." He went on to say "Naked people have little or no influence in society." That's why the world's top designers hope to influence the world by lending their frocks to stars. It's no accident that well-stocked wardrobe departments and well-paid stylists are an essential part of Hollywood. Actress Minnie Driver may have had it right when she said, "*You* have to sparkle, not your dress." She really did sparkle in that red Halston gown at the 1997 Oscars. But there's no doubt the dress helped.

Movie wardrobe designers have made such an impact that the multi-Oscar-winning designer Edith Head was rated number 50 on one list of the 100 most influential men and women of the movies, putting her ahead of such heavy hitters as Bette Davis (58), Steven Spielberg (82), and Mario Van Peebles (93). Edith designed for more than 1,000 movies, a job she said was about creating characters and moods through clothing. I know that there have been numerous times when my mood and the moods of those around me have been improved because of nothing more than what I was wearing.

Plotting Your Wardrobe

Whenever Edith got a script she would first break it down into what she called a "wardrobe plot." From there she would begin to figure out what those characters would wear as the story progressed. Use your life script as a guide in devising your personal wardrobe plot. Check back to your storyboard and think about what you will be wearing in those upcoming scenes. It can accelerate the realization of your dream. Consider the movie *To Catch a Thief.* Director Alfred Hitchcock asked Edith Head to dress Grace Kelly like a princess in the film. Reportedly Prince Rainier saw the movie and fell in love. She became a real princess after dressing the part. How can you start looking like a CEO, an anchorwoman, or a Supreme Court judge today?

Edith designed wardrobes so exactly that she envisioned that if the sound were to go off during one of her movies, viewers would still know about the characters just from the way they dressed. What are your clothes saying about you? What would you like them to start saying?

★ What is it about your character that you would like to emphasize? Openness? Softness? Creativity? Edith Head believed open and generous characters were complimented by "soft tones, clothes that look easy and that give a little." In her mind ". . . a collar that stands up around her face, or long cuffs were the hallmarks of a shy or rigid woman."

★ When it came to color Edith thought it had a greater impact on an outfit than the cut. "Lavender or purple and old lace" was how she envisioned a sweet old lady. Black was a color for vamps and "virginal white for a girl." When you find a color that really suits you, don't be afraid to weave it throughout your wardrobe in hats, scarves, and mittens.

★ On the worksheet labeled *Star Wardrobe Act III* sketch or use magazine clippings to illustrate the wardrobe you will be wearing in your dream scenes.

★ ★ ★ ★ ★ ★ ★ ★ ★ ★ ★ ★ ★ ★ ★ ★

Star Wardrobe Act III

★ ★ ★ ★ ★ ★ ★ ★ ★ ★ ★ ★ ★ ★ ★ ★

Editing

Pare down your wardrobe so that every single stitch that you have compliments your star style.

If you have any doubt about what should go, start asking yourself these questions: Would my favorite Hollywood star be caught wearing this slightly tattered dress? That well-worn jacket? This pilly sweater? That less than fresh sundress? If they wouldn't be caught wearing it, why should you? Get rid of all of those "extras" in your wardrobe that don't make you shine.

★ If you need help figuring out what needs to go, rely on costars and supporting players you trust. Or go back to the videotape and photos. Bad choices will scream at you.

★ Make a pile of all of the rest of the clothes that you are currently not wearing. They are likely to fall into some distinct categories: unflattering, "fat," or "thin" clothes. And then there is the heading of "What was I thinking?"

★ In the "unflattering" pile, do you see a pattern emerging? Do they all have empire waists? Are they all pleated? Are they all black? Are they all too young or too old looking? Too flashy or too subdued? If so, think twice the next time you are out shopping and avoid the same pitfalls.

★ Are the "fat" clothes a convenient excuse for you to pack on extra pounds? Whittle them down. If you have too great a collection of "thin" clothes you are just making your wardrobe fatter. When you get smaller you might want to wear a completely different style, so don't clog your wardrobe with those items.

★ This may sound like a strange question, but are there some clothes in your closet that you don't wear because you look too good in them? Perhaps you feel you get too much attention and you would rather not get so much praise. What did I say about being a spectator? Pull those star items front and center and sparkle in them as you should.

★ There may be some clothes that fit and look great on you but you forget about them because it so easy to slip into your regulars. Expand your wardrobe repertoire by making a wider range of your clothes active members of your wardrobe. One way is to store these items where you can see them. Then make a point of wearing one of your "sleepers" at least once a week.

★ You bought all that athletic gear because you have dreamed of living a more vigorous life. Perhaps you have a closet filled with gowns fit for glamorous events? Listen to your wardrobe. It may be calling you to act out your dreams. So start creating occasions to wear them. Find a place to go in those sweats, whether it's a spa or a public facility. Find a charitable event you and your romantic lead can support and then dust off your elbow-length gloves, your satin gown, and your tiara.

★ No matter how chic it is, no matter how many times it was featured on MTV, *Vogue,* or at awards shows, don't wear anything that makes you feel uncomfortable. Your discomfort will show on your face, whether it's a pair of shoes that pinch or jeans that are too snug.

★ Once you've edited your wardrobe, you can sell the clothing you don't want by either making a trip to the consignment store or peddle your wares through a garage sale. Remember, you are likely to get only a fraction of what you paid for it. You should also consider donating some of the items to a homeless shelter. Be on the lookout for programs that help women get back into the job market.

★ All your editing will help you identify the star players in your wardrobe, outfits you rely on for that all-important conference or that do-or-die job interview. Pull them together and analyze why those garments draw so many compliments. Is it because of the color? The cut? Is it because it's something different—perhaps more playful, more conservative, more colorful—than what you normally wear? Get a sequel. If the outfit is long gone out of the stores, go to a discount mall where they often feature last season's creations. Or have a dressmaker knock it off. When Joan Crawford found the perfect hat, she made multiple copies.

Personal Stylist

My mother is great to shop with because she reminds me of what I have too much of (black, lace, and leather). She has become my de facto stylist. She pushes me to try fresh fabrics and colors. She dresses me hipper than I dress myself. As I write this she just encouraged me to get yet another sale Vivienne Tam dress. And it was during her watch that I bought motorcycle boots, a paisley sarong, and a floor-length velvet coat trimmed with sienna faux fur (which goes with the Vivienne Tam dress).

Inevitably the most compliments are forthcoming when I wear her selections. If you don't have a mom like mine, and if you can't get on E! television's *Fashion Emergency,* cast for your own supporting players to help you with your wardrobe.

★ No stylist in your town and you don't have a mother like mine? Then examine the windows of your favorite shops where you live. Look carefully at the proportions, the accessories. See how the patterns and colors mix and match. My mother often buys complete outfits after taking cues from window dressing. But before you buy a thing first go to your closet and see what you have that is comparable to what you saw at the store.

★ While shooting a television report at the House of Dior in Paris I interviewed a woman who identified herself as Elizabeth Taylor's personal shopper. Word was she bought a vanload of clothing on behalf of her violet-eyed client. As she looked through the racks I began noticing that she had the same striking coloring as her Hollywood superstar boss. How convenient. Shop with girlfriends with similar coloring and builds. Use these doppelgängers to try on your selections so you can get an even better idea of how you'll look.

★ Find personal shoppers or sales associates who will be honest. You want them to tell you if those cargo pants make you look as though you are carrying too much cargo. Look for someone whose style complements yours. You also want folks who won't do the forty-yard dash when you need to make a return. Both of you can benefit from such a relationship. It could happen that the salesperson works in sportswear and you need formal wear. Enlist her to be on the lookout for your colors, your styles, and sales in every department.

★ Even if you don't have solicitous designers offering their clothing free, you can benefit from sales. When I posed for a photo in *The Washington Post* for a feature on chic residents of the nation's capital, everything from my black feathered hat to my Manolo Blahnik spikes were sale items.

★ Another route is to go to resale stores. I wore a used Yojhi Yamamoto to the West Coast premiere of Spike Lee's *He Got Game*. P.R. maven Makeda Smith always looks stunning at the events she coordinates at such varied venues as the Mondrian and the W Hotels where she interacts with the likes of

DMX, Carmen Electra, and Hugh Hefner. It's more than likely what she is wearing came from a resale shop. The last time I saw her at a party and complimented her on what she was wearing she told me she got it for all of eighteen dollars!

★ Use your fans as stylists. If you consistently get compliments about a certain color or cut of clothing take note.

★ I was visiting the atelier (fancy word for workshop) of a world-famous designer in Paris and saw photos scattered on desktops of the glamorous first ladies of film. Why were they there? For inspiration. Throw a few photos of chic women who inspire you around the closet to serve as silent stylists.

Lingerie

When Robert De Niro played Al Capone in the movie *The Untouchables* he went as far as wearing silk Sulka underwear. That's the same company that designed undergarments for the real Capone. For *Gone With the Wind* the right undergarments were so important that producer David O. Selznick reportedly stopped production as he waited for the arrival of French-made lingerie from Paris. Mind you these garments were not even visible on the screen. But Selznick is quoted as telling actress Olivia de Havilland that she "couldn't possibly play the part of Melanie . . . wearing the wrong undies." Well, you can't possibly play the part of a star without the right undies.

★ Don't make your undergarments an afterthought. There's a reason they call them foundation garments. A VPL (visible panty line), a bulging bra, and a sagging slip can ruin the impact of an otherwise stunning outfit.

★ Actress Marlene Dietrich favored a secret foundation known as a "soufflé." It was a thick bodysuit that gave her bosom and behind a youthful lift. They were delicate, custom-made numbers. It was such an essential part of her wardrobe that she had three dozen stand-bys. Look for the modern version of soufflés available at the lingerie department.

★ Even though he owned RKO movie studios, Trans World Airlines, and a substantial part of Nevada, Howard Hughes took time to make sure actress Jane Russell's chest was properly supported. Make sure your bra fits correctly. Since the last time you checked you might have lost or gained weight, nursed a baby, or done 1,000 bench presses.

★ When you find a bra that fits, do not hesitate to buy it in multiples especially if you have a Jane Russell–size bust.

★ Actress Debbie Reynolds once used a "nipper" to reduce her nineteen-inch waist to seventeen inches. Control tops designed without the hose attached can also shave off inches.

★ MGM actresses would soak their white underwear in tea to make it look more like flesh tone. It's always been frustrating to me that the color "nude" in the lingerie department does not match my cinnamon and nutmeg skin tones. So when I want to make my undergarments disappear under my clothing I dye them, mixing brown and gold.

★ When it comes to your nightly wardrobe, take a cue from soap opera actresses. You may be envious of the fantasy romance in their lives. It may have something to do with their luscious loungewear.

★ Buy robes that coordinate with your negligees. But they don't have to match. Then take your favorite Jean Harlow pose.

★ You know those perfume strips that fill your favorite magazines? Instead of throwing them away, tuck them into your lingerie drawer.

★ Lingerie seems to be vanishing. I have gone to awards ceremonies where it seems that on a clear day you could see *everything*. Not a bra or panty in sight. If you go for this look have a friend check you out to make sure you are PG rather than X-rated.

★ Don't forget to include slippers as part of your lingerie wardrobe, perhaps trimmed with marabou feathers. While you are at it get one of those satin eye masks like you see in the movies.

Special Occasions

Can a dress change your life? Ask actress and model Elizabeth Hurley. She showed up with onetime boyfriend actor Hugh Grant at the British premiere of *Four Weddings and a Funeral* wearing a sexy safety pin dress made by Gianni Versace. Soon after that Elizabeth vaunted into the celebrity stratosphere, snagging an Estée Lauder contract. She later made a star turn in the movie *Austin Powers: International Man of Mystery*. The right outfit at an important event such as a job interview, party, or maybe even a blind date can have a similar impact on your life.

★ Have plenty of stellar outfits in stock. That way you don't have to go on a frantic shopping spree after you are invited to appear on television or to present a report to the chairman of the board.

★ Designers often arrange for Hollywood stars to borrow clothing for special occasions. Can a friend loan you a frock for the evening? Be careful and considerate. When a coworker once asked to take one of my dresses for the night, I said, "Sure, but please dry clean it before you return it." This coworker balked. This is a no-brainer. Offer to clean the dress before you are asked.

★ When you go shopping bring along the shoes, stockings, and undergarments that would go with your dream dress. It's the only way you'll get a full appreciation of your total look. Many fancy boutiques will supply shoes for tryouts. But often they are not in contemporary styles and almost always they are in black.

★ You know how the groom is not supposed to see the bride on the day of the wedding until she comes down the aisle? Adopt that policy for other special days. Do not let your romantic lead see the nitty-gritty of your preparations for a big night out. Maintain your mystery. That's part of being a star. Actress Julia Roberts says she gets a hotel room separate from her romantic leading man when she is getting ready for glittery awards shows. That way she makes a dramatic entrance to perhaps her most important audience.

★ Beware of taking wardrobe cues from those candid photos featured in celebrity magazines. Talent agent Pat Quinn says Hollywood hopefuls see stars kicking it in St. Kitts or in the Hamptons in casual clothes, so they adopt that look for job interviews. Pat told me she couldn't believe it when a student who had just graduated from her alma mater, Yale, showed up for their first meeting in a ripped T-shirt and jeans. This new grad explained that he was just trying to dress Hollywood. Pat advised him that if he wanted to impress the other Yale alum he had set up meetings with he would be better advised to show up in khakis and a navy blazer. A successful television producer told Pat point blank that he would never hire a writer who came to a job interview wearing jeans. She passed along this advice to a couple of her writer clients who could not get work until they changed their wardrobes. Even creative Hollywood has limits on casualness. Of course, depending on the job, once you are hired you can bring out the Calvins and Levis.

Retail Therapy

Costumers have long known that clothing can produce a special kind of magic. "We create the illusion of changing the actors into what they are not," said doyenne designer Edith Head.

Gone With the Wind wardrobe designer Walter Plunkett used drab colors to underscore the illusion of dreariness in the movie's war scenes. For happy interludes he used bright hues for Scarlett and company. You may not have realized that when you were watching the film, but you probably felt it.

In real life the legendary entertainer Eartha Kitt once declared that she was not going to wear anything "that's not going to put me in a good mood." Look to your wardrobe to do the same.

★ The worse you feel, the better you must look. Pulling yourself together even though you are suffering through a cold or broken heart pays a lot of dividends. Of course you have the right to look so scary you make babies cry and dogs howl. But whenever I take charge of my appearance it always improves my mood because it gives me a sense of control.

★ If your battles of the day have left you feeling especially macho, switch to wearing the most feminine article in your wardrobe when you get home.

★ If the day has left you feeling out of control, find something that brings out your strength. (I'm not saying you should go back to wearing quarterback-size shoulder pads, but take a

look at how well Joan Collins's power outfits coordinated
with her powerful character in *Dynasty*.)

★ If your day has left you feeling sad, look into your wardrobe
for the most fun item. Maybe it's a hat, a pin, a T-shirt. Wear
it with a smile.

★ When I was living on the East Coast I got depressed every
winter. It was cabin fever. It was Seasonal Affective Disorder.
It was just plain SAD. After two miserable winters, I revised
my wardrobe plot by acquiring the most beautiful winter
clothing and accessories I could get my hands on. I stocked
my closet with everything from childish mittens to vinyl
gloves only a dominatrix would love. This therapy through
clothing helped me chase away the winter blues. In a matter
of time I actually began looking forward to winter.

As you put it all together, the grooming, the workouts, and the
wardrobe you'll immediately be able to see evidence of your star
power when you look in the mirror.

Now it's time to take a closer look at that mirror and the other
things on your set so that you can sprinkle some stardust on your
surroundings.

Too low they build, who build beneath the stars.
— EDWARD YOUNG

★

CHAPTER NINE

Live the Part

Create Stellar Sets, Soundtracks,
Props, and Craft Services

Let's say you're watching an interview with a multimillionaire who is talking about the joys of having so much money. Wouldn't you question what was really going on with her bottom line if the backdrop was a dirty, decaying house, haphazardly decorated with orange crates and bricks? Conversely, if you saw a down and out person talking about how rough life was as she stood in her own immaculate living room elaborately outfitted with museum-quality antiques, you'd probably think twice about giving her a handout.

If a stranger were to walk into your place today what conclusions about you would she draw from the set you live in, the music you listen to, the props that fill your life and the food that you eat? Would she assume you are a star? If not, why not? It's time to create a stellar environment to compliment your radiant life.

On Set

When I lived in Washington, D.C., a few years ago, my life was pretty spartan. The furnishings in my apartment consisted of nothing more than a futon, a lamp, a television, and a rug remnant. It's no wonder I felt depressed from the moment I entered my place. My surroundings were just a step above basic shelter. Because I was on the road so much I didn't think my interiors mattered much. I was wrong.

Flash-forward four years to my current set in California. Come into my living room now and you will find a Mexican antique chandelier hanging above the dinner table; go around the corner to the bathroom and you'll find African masks accented with gold; if you make the turn to my bedroom you'll find a bed covered with plush pillows (all purchased on sale, by the way). The nesting bug got me, and the pleasant environment that I created as a result in some ways saved my life. During that time, I was smack in the middle of a drama with a workplace villain. My daily dealings with her were draining, but no matter what I had been through during my day, the moment I turned the key to my door, I smiled. Not only did my furnishings reflect my tastes, they helped me shine and provided comfort.

Television and movie productions can get away with using beautiful façades. Only cast and crew know that stunning scenes are propped up by plywood. Your set cannot be so one-dimensional. Your starring role requires you to pay attention to every angle on your set. Just as the elaborate, futuristic sets for the movie *Blade Runner* made us believe that we were watching the future, your set can go a long way in making visitors believe they are in the presence of a star. Of course the person you'll want to impress most on set, on your set, will always be you.

Get Ready, Set, Go for It

★ Spend a weekend renting at least half a dozen movies (Blockbuster is not paying me to say this) that feature the kind of décor that fits your starring role. You don't have to follow the plotline of the films. In fact you have my permission to turn the volume down. What I do want you to do is to study the set design. Look to see how the set designer handled window treatments, entertainment and communication centers, and lighting. What kind of accessories did they use? What are the dominant colors and materials? If your set calls for sleek, futuristic furniture rent *Blade Runner, Star Trek,* and any *Star Wars* movies. If you are going for a contemporary, eclectic look, check out the movie *Diva* and almost any film made by Pedro Aldomovar or Tim Burton.

★ Clipping magazine articles is helpful but there are other ways to audition decorating styles. You can get the full effect by seeing a dream room in 3-D. If there's a standout hotel (Victorian, modern, belle époque) that you really admire, it's easy enough to go and check out the lobby, the restaurants, and the courtyards and such. If you want a look at one of the rooms, but you're not staying there, no problem. Advise the front desk you'd like to see a room. You don't have to tell them why. A bellman may be required to take you up. Tip him a buck. Such a deal, for previewing a room of your dreams.

★ Whenever possible take your own photographs or videotape what you like. You may not be able to pinpoint exactly what it is you admire when you are looking at something in person. Capturing the image will help you analyze your tastes. Even if your artistic skills are minimal, make sketches of how you would envision your dream room. Keep a collection of the sketches and photos together as you come up with your own decorating master plan.

★ And don't be afraid of mixing styles. One of the most unusual combinations I have encountered was at the St. James Hotel in Bouliac, France. The décor in this postmodern hotel is French country meets Zen.

★ Let your environment reflect your interests. Author and script consultant Dr. Linda Seger lets everyone who comes to her office know how much she likes the wild, wild West. The room is decorated with everything from chaps to slickers. What hobbies can you put on display?

★ Before actress Lindsay Wagner films one of her car commercials, producers make sure they select a vehicle that looks good "on" the actress. Just as you choose clothing that is complimentary to your coloring, find furnishings that go with your skin tones. Realize that you are going to "wear" your house more than that Donna Karan suit or Byron Lars play dress. The movie *Waiting to Exhale* is an example of a set that coordinated beautifully with the skin tones of the movie's stars.

★ Look to your wardrobe for ideas. If you could magically turn your favorite clothes into furnishings, how would they look? What are the proportions, colors, and textures that immediately come to mind? Think of how the clothing of Ralph Lauren fits perfectly with the home furnishings he designs. In both realms the lines are traditional. If you find that you are more expressive in what you wear, turn up the volume where you live.

★ The excuse that you don't have enough space to create a star setting just doesn't cut it. Think of the beauty and elegance of a jewelry box. It too is small. Jewelry boxes are often covered in rich, dark velvet. When you see one you immediately know that it contains something that's valuable. Aren't you more precious than any diamond? In decorating a small space think of how you can give it the "jewel box" effect. Begin by selecting rich materials.

★ Set up your interiors to represent scenes you would like to play out in the rooms of your home. Make these tableaus so powerful that anyone taking a casual tour will immediately get it. The candles, the bath pillow, and the bubble bath in your bathroom can designate a relaxation zone. The books and reading and magnifying glasses can indicate the spot where you read. The games perpetually set up in the den can be visual triggers for playtime with the kids. Turn these scenes into "visiting exhibitions" that you can easily change whenever you switch bath oils or buy new books or board games.

★ Stars always seem to have names for their estates. Tara was Scarlett O'Hara's residence in *Gone With the Wind*. Audrey Hepburn called her Swiss villa La Paisible "the peaceful place." What do you call chez toi? Where I live would not qualify as an estate, but I still have a name for it. I call it Hermitage, which means a secluded dwelling—a safe haven. Make up a stellar title for your place. Then live up to it.

Lighting

A legendary sex symbol on a publicity tour was scheduled for an early morning television show, but before this shapely celebrity would be ready for her close-up, something had to be done about the lighting. And she caused enough of a ruckus for the crew to know that she was serious.

Word is that legendary funny lady Lucille Ball did not demand better lighting. Instead she came up with her own way of disguising it. The Lucy that we loved was known for wearing hats during guest appearances. She never knew what the lighting situation would be, but her hat brims would diffuse the ill effects of overhead lighting.

Actress Barbara Bain did not have such worries when she appeared in the television series *Mission: Impossible.* I once heard her say that as the only female star of the show at the time, she was the subject of an edict from the producers to never allow a shadow on her face. There was even an episode of *Seinfeld* that focused on the alternately flattering and unflattering lighting that bathed the face of one of Jerry's love interests.

Do an experiment right now. Take the shade off one of your lamps and position yourself in a place where you can see yourself in the mirror. For the most dramatic results do this in a darkened area with a high-wattage bulb. Hold the lamp above you. You should see shadows, just as you see them at high noon. Next, move the lamp to where you normally have your lamp placed, and then hold the lamp beneath you. In that position you may well end up looking like Bela Lugosi. Not pretty. Make an assessment of the lighting scheme of your home and office. Eyeball it with a mirror. Better yet have a record of it by getting someone to videotape it. If you are going to be in the spotlight, make it flattering.

★

You may think that lighting is only relevant in Hollywood, but you can dramatically improve your appearance right this moment by adjusting the wattage in your life. Part of the warm glow that you are bathed in every time you and your romantic lead are nibbling strawberries at your favorite restaurant is due to the lighting. You'll feel it, too, when your skin takes on the greenish pallor of fluorescent lights. It's time to see the light.

★ Design your lighting to mimic the warm, soft light you see at sunrise or sunset. If you have ever watched one of the behind-the-scenes *Sports Illustrated* swimsuit issue specials you may have noticed that most of the photos are taken either at sunrise or sunset. You will not find any photos taken in the harsh, direct midday sunlight. I figure what's good for supermodels is good for me. Dimmers, indirect light, and tinted bulbs will help you create flattering lighting.

★ Further familiarize yourself with good lighting by renting a few films. Black-and-white movies with the likes of Greta Garbo and Marlene Dietrich feature outrageously good lighting. Spike Lee's films have masterful warm and soft lighting, especially those from the early years. More shouts for the lighting directors who worked on the movie *How Stella Got Her Groove Back* and *Waiting to Exhale.* You can also educate yourself on lighting by visiting your local museum. The masters really knew how to light. Look at the luminous subjects of Rembrandt, Ingres, and Vermeer.

★ Now that you know what's good, you'll be more sensitive to bad lighting design. Are you confronted with the feared, unflattering overhead fluorescent lighting? You don't have to pay for an expensive makeover. One solution is to switch off the existing light and bring in table lamps.

Artwork

Whether you are hanging Picassos or postcards, a Léger or a lithograph, find ways to include art on your set. With so many sources of art available you don't have to have a movie star's wallet to assemble your own collection. Enhance the walls of your set with everything from reproductions to flea market finds.

★ Don't install art that doesn't give you a visual buzz. I appreciate all kinds of art, but all of the art I own makes me feel good.

★ Dot your set with inspirational hangings, pillows, and writings. Your eyes are sure to spy one of them just when you need a boost.

★ Create art from places you love. Something as simple as stamps or currency from locales you have visited can be turned into a work of art back home.

★ If you are having trouble figuring out how to frame your artwork, get tips from the masters. Go to a gallery or museum. Look for pieces with similar colors and proportions. Also pay attention to the placement of the artwork and the lighting. When framing a parody painting of me as Mona Lisa I looked at a photo I had taken of the real thing as a reference point for making my selection.

Temporary Sets

Your home is not your only set. There is also your car, your office, your hotel room. Even Barbra Streisand's *dressing rooms* are filled with antiques and paintings. No matter how small your office space or hotel room, you can make it a reflection of you. Include photos of the people and places you love. Post copies of your favorite inspirational sayings. If you're going to be staying somewhere for a while, bring your own pillows, blankets, vases, and planters if you can. You might even want to rearrange the furniture so that it resembles your favorite room at home.

★

Soundtrack

Have you ever seen one of those television segments concerning the impact of music scores? The story inevitably begins with a series of scenes that are shown without music. The same scenes are then replayed with music. What a difference the melodies make! Scary scenes are all the more terrifying, carefree scenes lighter, and the romantic interludes all the more loving. Some filmmakers believe that a single song is as powerful as a couple pages of script. A personal soundtrack can enhance the scenes of your life as well.

Star musician Ray Charles said, "There's something about music that's healing. Unless you're about dead, music'll do something for you." And if you won't take Ray's word for it, study after study has shown that there is in fact "a biology of music." Researchers in Massachusetts found that male musicians had significantly larger brains than their less tuned-in counterparts. Classically trained musicians at Beth Israel Deaconess Medical Center in Boston discovered that the area of the brain called the cerebellum was about 5 percent larger in men who had extensive musical training. So I guess music can really blow your mind.

Even babies can get their groove on. A Florida State University study found that preemies could gain immediate effects from music. Researchers found that premature babies exposed to music gained weight faster, were calmer, and used oxygen more efficiently.

Use music to help you thrive.

Theme Songs

★ Is there a theme in the lyrics you listen to? If your music library is filled with "somebody done somebody wrong" songs, is there any wonder you think people are out to get you? Edit out the misery and find another beat.

★ Tune into success. A working Hollywood actress I know heads to her auditions listening to the uplifting music of the Sounds of Blackness. By the time she gets to her destination she is invigorated and ready to win the part. Go to that job interview with your own victory music.

★ Is there a golden time that can be brought back to life with music? I'm not talking about being a musical neo-Norma Desmond who is stuck in the past. But what better way to evoke pleasant memories than to rerun the sounds of the favorite times in your life? Remember that trek you made to Katmandu after college when you listened to the songs of the Pointer Sisters? Hit replay. Maybe your college-age kids will enjoy the songs as you recall past happiness in the Himalayas.

★ Use music to accompany that big project you are working on. Let's say you are helping with a charity dinner and the theme is Versailles. Listen to the music of that period as you arrange the seating plan. Or perhaps you're working on a term paper on South Africa. Have Miriam Makeba or Ladysmith Black Mombazo playing in the background.

★ Incorporate sounds into your life that make you feel like a winner. You're a performer? Find recordings of applause, especially on live albums. Applause can be useful, even if you aren't in entertainment. Crank up the clapping whenever you need a lift.

House Music

The entire New York City apartment of tv personality Katie Couric is wired with a state-of-the-art sound system. She believes "a home with music is a really happy place." It may not be possible for you to do an electronic makeover but you can still find ways to fill your house with harmony. Try to have radios and CD players positioned throughout the house and in the garden.

★ Program music to suit the different moods of the different areas of your home. Department stores do it all the time. When I was going through racks of Dolce & Gabbana at a Beverly Hills store I couldn't help but sing along with RuPaul's "Supermodel (You Better Work)." Then I went to another floor where I noted that classical music was served up along with the St. John knits. Retailers see music as an integral part of creating a lifestyle. Don't just leave it to them. Try jazzy music for your kitchen. Consider upbeat tunes for your entrance. Your call for what you want to hear in your bedroom.

★ Eateries are paying a lot of attention to dinner music, according to *The New York Times.* Tunes by Ella Fitzgerald and Louis Armstrong are almost as popular in New York City as chicken and steak entrees. One innovative East Village restaurant hired a live disc jockey to serve up the music. Vonda Shepard, the featured singer-songwriter on the *Ally McBeal* television show is so sound sensitive that she will leave a restaurant in the "middle of a wonderful meal if the music is bad." Pipe some music into your dining room. But keep it slow. Some experts say fast music will make you eat at the same pace.

★ Even opera singer Placido Domingo says he does some of his best singing in the shower. I just read about another musical artist who has actually rigged his shower with a mike wired to his recording system. Waterproof radios are available for your shower so you can have accompaniment the next time you sing in the stall.

★ Tune up your clean up. Raquel Welch is known to have put on Elvis Presley when she was cleaning house during the early stages of her career. Why not try playing The King or Queen Latifah as you tidy up?

Tuning in on Location

A former colleague would always sit in the television newsroom wearing earphones. I always assumed he was listening to recordings of his interviews. It took me weeks to discover that in the midst of the newsroom madness, he had carved out an oasis. In fact he was listening to music as he wrote his scripts while police scanners and ringing phones blasted the rest of us.

Actress Lana Turner had a more elaborate way of bringing music to work. She had a supporting player on staff whose job responsibilities included keeping her ears filled with music. The sultry siren was married seven times, and as you might imagine she favored romantic music. Find ways to take tunes with you on location.

★ Bring a boom box to the hospital. Dr. Joyce Brothers reports that when a critical care unit piped in classical music, one doctor found that ninety minutes of the music produced the same effect as ten milligrams of Valium.

★ An increasing number of hotel rooms come equipped with CD or cassette players. Find out about your setup before you take off.

★ When you are in the water, catch some soundwaves. Go swimming with a waterproof portable radio or cassette player.

Playlist

You'll get an extra push as you read this book by listening to songs that harmonize with the theme of each chapter. It will reinforce the messages. If you need some help in figuring out exactly what to tune into I offer the following playlist.

Introduction: "Shining Star" (Earth, Wind and Fire)

Chapter 1, Create the Role of a Lifetime: "All Star" (Smash Mouth); "Everybody Is a Star" (Sly and the Family Stone)

Chapter 2, Pre-production: "Make It Happen" (Mariah Carey)

Chapter 3, What Is Your Motivation? "Stand!" (Sly and the Family Stone)

Chapter 4, Your Long-Term Life Script: "Do You Know Where You're Going To?" (Diana Ross)

Chapter 5, Your Short-Term Life Script: "Day by Day" (Soundtrack from *Godspell*); "Beautiful Day" (U2)

Chapter 6, Editing: "Accentuate the Positive" (Bing Crosby)

Chapter 7, Costars, Supporting Players, Fans, and Villains: "Every Kinda People" (Robert Palmer); "Wind Beneath My Wings" (Bette Midler); "People Make the World Go 'Round" (Temptations); "Shower the People You Love with Love" (James Taylor)

Chapter 8, Get Ready for Your Close-up: "Unpretty" (TLC); "Physical" (Olivia Newton-John); "Supermodel" (RuPaul); "I'm Beautiful" (Bette Midler); "Smile" (Vitamin C)

Chapter 9, Live the Part: "Celebrate Me Home" (Kenny Loggins); "Slave to the Rhythm" (Grace Jones); "Music" (Madonna); "My Favorite Things" (Julie Andrews)

Chapter 10, On Hiatus: "Just Coolin" (La Vert); "Treat Myself" (Stevie Wonder); "Fly Away" (Lenny Kravitz)

Chapter 11, Crisis Points: "Don't Rain on My Parade" (Barbra Streisand); "I Will Survive" (Gloria Gaynor); "You Can't Always Get What You Want" (Rolling Stones); "Climb Every Mountain" (Soundtrack from *The Sound of Music*)

Chapter 12, Happy Endings: "You Can Make It If You Try" (Sly and the Family Stone); "I'm Going All the Way" (Sounds of Blackness); "Here's to Life" (Shirley Horn)

★

Vocalizing

So it's not in your budget to get your latest favorite CD and you
have not been able to figure out how to download music from the
Internet. I have a solution that won't cost you a thing and we are
talking user-friendly. Use your God-given vocal chords.

Singing can go a long way in rehabilitating your mood. Dr.
Norman Vincent Peale recommended singing two songs a day as
a surefire way to chase away the blues. Don't be a spectator when
it comes to the music in your life.

In the movie *Flawless* a stroke patient played by Robert De Niro
improves his speech by taking singing lessons from a flamboyant,
cross-dressing neighbor. The storyline is based on real-life success
stories. Doctors are in fact using music to rehabilitate stroke patients. Amazingly researchers have found that some stroke patients who have lost their ability to speak continue to sing!

★ Script consultant and author Linda Seger has a song to sing
for every mood. "I Have Confidence" from *The Sound of
Music* is what she sings when she wants to cheer up, an appropriate choice considering the genre of her choice is musical
comedy. Come up with selections to suit your moods.

★ Africans and African-Americans have a history of singing
while working. It doesn't matter which culture club you belong to; when you need an extra push to complete a task, sing
it, Sister.

★ Cheer yourself by singing songs from your youth. Lullabies
can be especially soothing.

★ For a natural stress reliever Don Campbell, the author of *The
Mozart Effect,* prescribes three minutes of humming. He
compares it to getting a "massage for your head" from the inside out.

Props

Designer sunglasses. Stretch limousines. Diamond necklaces. They are all props favored by Hollywood royalty. The prop of choice in the country of my birth is a horse's tail. It is a status symbol for chieftains. That's why you may have seen photos of various African presidents and prime ministers clutching this equine prop. One of the attractions of props, both in Africa and America, is that they help define images.

They can even improve performance. Actor Cary Grant wasn't happy with the props that were going to be featured in a library scene in the movie *That Touch of Mink*. So on the day of filming he arrived with boxes filled with items from his own study. Costar Doris Day says those props helped him nail the scene. The right props can help you nail the scenes of your life by adding shine to your environment.

Props can be as lavish as a Christofle caviar bowl or as simple as a colorful postage stamp. The only requirement is that they bring points of light into your life. Writing out your bills with a silver fountain pen instantly makes the process less burdensome. Adding up the restaurant tip won't seem like such a chore if your calculator is encrusted in faux jewels. Brushing your teeth with a brush you plucked from a gold-flecked antique glass brings glamour to personal hygiene.

Too often it seems that our best props are stored away in dark closets. They only see light on special occasions or when company comes over. Starring in your own life means the good dishes, the crystal vases, and your best towels are all part of your everyday life script. To paraphrase the hair color ad, aren't you worth it?

Around the House

★ Invest the most in the props you use the most. Think about upgrading utilitarian versions of items you use frequently.

Replace that cracked soap dish with a gleaming crystal one. Exchange that dingy plastic flowerpot for a porcelain one in bright blue. Get rid of those bricks you are using as bookends and replace them with the real thing.

★ Make a survey of all the containers in your home, with an eye on editing. Get rid of anything that's grimy, unappealing, or cheap looking.

★ What do you use to store your sugar, flour, and pasta? Finding attractive repositories for your dry goods adds to their flavor. Whatever you get should reflect the set you have created in your kitchen. You could try silver-plated containers or hunt down one-of-a-kind antiques at your local consignment shop or flea market.

★ Find cues on storage ideas by making a visit to a museum. Study the paintings of days gone by and discover how people in the past used props. Be on special lookout for crafts of your ancestors. If your African forefathers and mothers used beaded baskets to serve food, consider filling your table with them instead of porcelain china.

★ Bring some pleasure to washing the dishes by squirting your liquid soap out of a beautiful dispenser.

★ Get one of those designer, stainless-steel sink stoppers. They come in whimsical designs that include hearts.

★ Make watching time go by more enjoyable by getting calendars that reflect your character. A nurse I encountered on a location in Portland, Oregon, takes it a step further by framing hers.

★ Surround yourself with props that remind you of happy childhood memories. Maybe it's that worn teddy bear. Or it could be your first basketball. Or a bag of marbles.

★ If you spend a lot of time on the phone, make it a prop that brings out your character. A breathtaking variety is available, from sleek little black numbers to Baroque gold-plated ones.

★ Fancy hotels often supply a phone in every room. It's a luxury I have long enjoyed on the road. Why not bring it home and hook up phones in the kitchen, in the bathroom, in the laundry room? Actress Ali MacGraw says when she was married to Hollywood producer Bob Evans he had thirty-two phones ringing throughout the house.

★ Make banishing bad breath a glamorous business. Store your mouthwash in a beautiful glass container. Caution! Only grown-ups should have access to the bottle. Avoid crystal because of the possibility of lead poisoning.

★ Props without price tags can be priceless. Actress Isabella Rossellini's bathroom sink is circled with stones, all meaningful. One was from a Swedish island where her mother, Ingrid Bergman, would summer. Another came from Stromboli where it seems her parents fell in love. Shells collected from Palm Beach and South Beach ring my bathtub. Start making similar cost-free collections of happy memories.

Flower Power

Instead of joining Barbra in a chorus of *You Don't Bring Me Flowers* anymore, get some for yourself. I used to fuss over the fact that I did not have enough flowers in my life. Of course, I expected to receive them from romantic leading men. Then I remember very distinctly standing by a flower stand in Paris and seeing an older woman who looked to be of modest means, beaming as she bought herself a bunch of flowers. Then it clicked. Duh. I can buy flowers for myself. Plants and flowers are among the favorite props of many stars, including Oprah Winfrey and Bette Midler. A makeup artist told me one superstar has one person in her employ whose job it is to carry a flower around. Whenever she needs a lift, that person is beckoned so that she can have a sniff. Sounds bizarre. But isn't it better to get a buzz from a daffodil than a Jack Daniel's?

In his book *8 Weeks to Optimum Health,* Dr. Andrew Weil prescribes ordering up fresh flowers once a week. It's time for you to incorporate petal power into your life.

★ The flowers don't have to cost a fortune. I frequently buy them from my supermarket for ten dollars. That's just half the fun. Then I enjoy the ritual of arranging them in a crystal vase or a simple glass pitcher. If you need help in making arrangements, there are lots of books out there. You can take classes. Or get a photo of the most beautiful bouquet you have ever seen. Take it to your florist, even if that florist happens to be at your grocery store. Ask for tips on how you can replicate the look. Go home with photo and clippers in hand and start to create.

★ Another way to save money on flowers is to buy varieties known to last a long time. One enduring example is protea.

★ Fruits and vegetables can stand in for flowers: lemons, squash, pomegranates. Plus they do double duty because you can eat them, too.

★ Don't just think about what you see above the rim. Submerge apples, blueberries, or cranberries in the water to add to your arrangement. And you don't always have to put flowers in

water. Just for fun at a party I used orange juice instead of
H_2O to add drama and more orange to an arrangement of
marigolds and daisies.

★ One of the favorite flower bouquets I ever received happened
to be of those long lasting protea, a flower that grows in my
ancestral homeland of South Africa. Before you buy yourself
flowers, do some investigative work about your background.

★ Choose foliage to decorate your set that is consistent with
your starring role. For example, if you're a warm-blooded
island girl/woman set your sultry self up with plants
reminiscent of the tropics.

★ Floral arrangements can go in every room in the house. In the
movie *How Stella Got Her Groove Back* I spotted flowers in
every room from the bathroom to the kitchen.

★ My version of Joan Crawford's "No wire hangers!" dictum is
no fake flowers—ever. They never shine as brightly as the
real thing. Better you should gather some dandelions or buy a
single rose than to get a bouquet of the faux stuff.

★ Dry the petals of an especially meaningful bouquet. Then
make up a personalized potpourri. An arts and crafts store
will tell you what you need to complete the mix.

Personal Props

★ Collect props that reflect your passion. You're a writer? Be on
the lookout for Underwood typewriters, fountain pens, and
inkwells. You'll be reminded of what you love every time
you glance at those items.

★ Use props as a visual aid to help remind you of your motivation. You are moonlighting in order to take that once-in-a-

lifetime trip to South Africa; keep a mask from the Xhosa tribe within your eyeline at work. Finger it whenever you are wondering why in the world you are working so hard.

★ Props can also be a symbol of your triumph over challenges. I am woefully nearsighted. Plus my eyeballs are shaped in an irregular way because of an astigmatism. But I so enjoy wearing glasses that people actually are surprised to find out that I have to wear them. I have quite a fanciful collection, thanks to the avante-garde tastes of my optician brother.

★ In actress Kim Novak's heyday, Columbia studios decreed that the color purple would dominate the actress's wardrobe. Keeping in character, Kim would send out purple thank-you notes. You don't have any studio telling you what to do, but if you love animal print clothing and furniture, buy matching stationery. It will make the memory of you linger, which was exactly what the studio chiefs had in mind for Kim.

★ Stop carrying your medication around in crumpled aluminum foil. Raise your spirits by storing your pills in something more elegant. Judith Leiber makes beautiful fancy pill cases. My neighborhood drugstore has an impressive array at a lower price. Until recently I thought they were pretty much just for women. When a beloved male family member was battling a terminal illness I discovered many macho ones as well, including the one I selected for him that was trimmed in leather.

★ Bring glamour to prophylactics and your monthly cycle. Gucci actually makes tampon and condom holders. The Rodeo Drive store tells me that both items have been very popular.

★ You have evening shoes, evening bags, evening clothes. Why not get evening glasses? They don't have to be covered with gewgaws and sequins; just make them dressy. I wore rimless ones with rhinestone accents to the Emmys one year. Heavy black frames or faux tortoise shell would not have coordinated with my dress.

Business Props

★ She could turn the world on with her smile, but what got my attention on *The Mary Tyler Moore Show* was the single rose Mary always had planted on her desk. Bring a flower to your office set.

★ Which office supplies do you use every day? Post-its? Tape? Staples? Select props to compliment your needs. My home office includes a silver-plated Post-it holder and tape dispenser, as well as a pewter crocodile-shaped stapler. They make work more fun.

★ You're a computer nerd? There is a wealth of computer props. Personalize your mouse pad with a photo of a loved one. Try a leather-covered computer disc holder. Put a frame around your monitor.

★ Did you have to fumble through your purse the last time someone asked you for a business card? Then you produced a mutilated or crumpled one? It's time for you to get a prop known as a cardholder. They come in a variety of styles. I've seen them decorated with peacock feathers or plated with silver. Make a ritual out of presenting your card.

★ Business cards are such an important prop that actor Robert De Niro had them specially printed up for his role in the movie *Falling in Love*. Mind you, they were never seen on film. He just wanted to carry them around in his pocket.

That made it all the more puzzling when a freelance journalist who once worked for a major weekly newsmagazine handed me one of his cards recently. I could see the perforations where the card had been torn from a sheet. Immediately it made me wonder about how well things were going for him since he left the magazine. Do you want people to have a similar impression? I don't recommend computer generated cards, especially the ones with the cloying prefabricated graphics. You can get personalized business cards printed for as little as twenty dollars. The quality of your business cards says a lot about you. You know you are on the right track when you get positive comments when you hand them out. Cards featuring color, metallic, and parchment paper have elicited the best response when I have exchanged them over the years. How can you make yours shine?

★ Also pay attention to your stationery. The recipient of your letter will begin to form an opinion of you from the moment they see the envelope. I did not respond to a letter inviting me to take part in a movie because the letterhead looked so unprofessional. I thought if that's how the letter looks, I have to question the quality of the production.

On Wheels

★ A car can seem like your second home, especially living in Los Angeles. Decorate it like one. You have those plush pillows on your sofa. Why not plop some in your car? Perhaps animal print. Add a chenille throw while you are at it.

★ Limousines are not just for taking Hollywood stars to premiers and awards shows. This prop on wheels can be therapeutic. Hire one to take a shut-in for a tour of the city. Or line one up to take a sick friend to an especially painful visit to the doctor.

★ Washington, D.C., boasts one of the cleanest metro systems I have ever seen. That's why it wasn't much of a surprise to see riders in tuxedos and evening gowns during former President Clinton's first inaugural. One of the reasons the metro is so clean is that food and drink are forbidden. If you want to keep your car sparkling, consider issuing the same edict.

★ Instead of using those cardboard Christmas trees, keep your car smelling wonderful by stocking it with potpourri. I keep mine in a green velvet bag tucked into a side pocket. The scent cheers me from the time I open the car door.

Getting In and Out of a Limousine

Even if the paparazzi are not snapping your every move you still want to look graceful as you maneuver your way out of your limousine. First consider your wardrobe. Low necklines and high hemlines can get you into trouble.

So now you are ready to make your exit. The first thing to do is slide to the very edge of your seat nearest the door. Lower your head. Swing out your legs (keeping them together as best as you can) to the outside of the car. Use your arms to lift yourself out. If you have someone standing there to help you, step up lightly and take his or her hand. And smile. That's even if no one is taking your picture.

What about getting back into a limousine? Well, never go in head first, unless you believe your backside is your best side. Besides backing into your stretch will make it easier to get a last look at any adoring fans.

Use your arms to steady you as your rear hits the seat, then swing in your legs.

So remember, legs out first, when you are making an exit. Bring your behind in first, when you are making an entrance. This modus operandi will look equally graceful when getting in and out of a sports utility vehicle or compact.

★

Craft Services

The sport utility vehicle snaked its way around side streets to the concert venue. At the destination the audience was starting to assemble. Seated inside the moving SUV were the members of the band who would soon take the stage. Behind the wheel was the road manager, to his right the band's bassist. I was in the back seat with the group's lead singer and songwriter. Even though I had known him for a couple of years and had heard him on the radio, this was the first time I would see him perform. Although I have covered various concerts in the past, this behind-the-scenes view was new to me. For the most part the mood was pretty low key. Then suddenly an urgent phone call went out, cellular phone to backstage. The atmosphere became intense. Then a critical question.

"Are you *sure* there is vegetarian food?"

Go backstage at almost any concert, movie, or television production and you'll see how important craft services are to the well-being of cast and crew. It's why chefs are as essential to a Hollywood star's staff as a personal assistant. And it's the reason I overheard a budget-strapped movie director say that she could scrimp on everything else but the food.

The folks in craft services fuel performers with everything from Fuji apples to mineral water. Why not take a tasty clue from their often finicky eating habits? Have your fill of all that is good. Delight your nose, hands, eyes, and mouth. It was the irrepressible bon vivant Auntie Mame who said that life is a banquet but most poor suckers are starving. Make sure you are well fed.

Presentation

I don't have any scientific data to back this up, but I believe that one of the reasons the French are generally so thin, in spite of the buttery croissants and rich crème brûlée, is because of the presentation of the food. It's so beautiful that you have to stop, look, and admire it. Then you eat. It's so much easier to scarf down junk food with nary a thought. Think about it. Binge eaters don't even look at their food. They can eat a loaf of bread straight out of a plastic bag.

Slow down and enjoy the view. The French and food stylists are not the only ones who can create pretty plates. You can, too.

★ If you are into clothing and not cooking, then think of your meals as a basic black dress. Garnishes serve as accessories to dress up your meals. Besides, basil is a lot cheaper than Fendi or Prada. Check out magazines, fancy restaurants, and those TV food shows for ideas.

★ Presentation always gets a great deal of attention at every spa that I have ever visited. I think it's their way of getting away with serving you less. Instead of just taking home spa products, think about how you can add their presentation methods to your own meals.

★ Sometimes just the way you cut food makes all the difference. You can get that fancy gizmo you saw advertised on an infomercial. But also experiment with a regular knife. Bring sparkle by doing something as simple as cutting your carrots, celery, or potatoes at a different angle.

Food as Therapy

★ Food can surely be therapy, but I'm not talking about Dr. Häagen-Dazs. Just as I prescribed myself a cheery winter wardrobe to help me get over the winter blues, I also started searching the supermarket aisles for sunshine. I found it in mangos. At times I even indulged in having two a day. Every bite—pure sunlight. Look for healthy feel-good foods.

★ Actress Alicia Silverstone was really not so clueless in the movie *Clueless.* She advised women to have something baking in the oven when expecting a visit from a romantic lead. That way the aroma would hit him the moment he walked in the door. Why just save the good smell for costars? Use this form of kitchen aromatherapy to greet you at your own door. Turn on the slow cooker or breadmaker before you take off in the morning. Just be sure to follow the proper safeguards.

★ Whip up memories as you make your meals. Prepare foods from the best scenes of your life. Are there (healthy) foods that remind you of a happy place, a beloved costar, or a favorite set? When you are dining on those treats make sure you make a conscious effort to feast on the good memories associated with those foods.

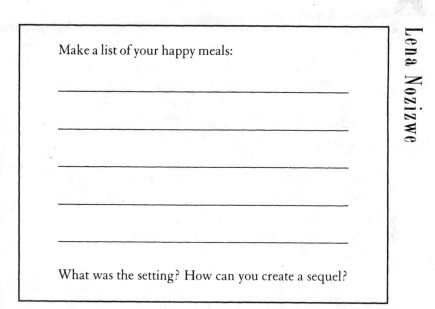

Make a list of your happy meals:

_____

_____

_____

_____

_____

What was the setting? How can you create a sequel?

Table Props

There's a television researcher I used to work with who ate Chinese take-out on a regular basis. She always impressed me because she never ate out of the cartons. Oh no. Instead, she always served herself lunch at the office on china. She added flavor to her meal without adding calories.

Director Alfred Hitchcock had a similar notion of gentility. Actress Eva Marie Saint says he would never let her drink her coffee from a Styrofoam cup while on set. He would insist she be served on china.

Television producer Cathy Stanley has taken this philosophy home. My one-time assistant may not know exactly what she will eat every night, but she knows what she will eat it on. She tells me that after a day on the set of Black Entertainment Television she serves her evening meal on crystal and sterling. Another friend presents his meals on Hermès plates, Daum crystal, and Christofle utensils placed on Pratesi placemats—*everyday!* For him there is no distinction between the "good" dishes and the everyday variety.

★ Collect props to compliment your cooking proclivities. You eat a lot of Chinese? Find some mother of pearl or silver-plated chopsticks. Is corn on the cob frequently on your menu? Get those fancy cob holders. Is African cuisine your favorite? Find some beaded baskets to serve it up on instead of china. But don't get that beautiful asparagus server if you don't like the green stalks.

★ Don't refrain from entertaining because you don't have a dozen matching place settings. Collect mismatching but coordinating china from antique stores and flea markets. It will actually make your table look more charming than all that matchy-matchy stuff.

★ Plastic and wood serving trays are okay. But there is a certain gorgeousness to serving breakfast in bed on a silver tray. I fell in love with an oversize version that came with room service at a hotel in southwest France. Memories of that trip resurface every time I serve food on my own silver tray.

★ If you are known for collecting stars, unicorns, or roses look for corresponding props. That would include star-shaped baking pans, unicorn molds, and rose cookie cutters.

★ If you are at a fancy dinner and are getting lost in all the props, discreetly look to the most sophisticated guest at the table. Use her to prompt you on which utensils to use. You can also get tips from eating scenes in the movies, especially English epics, about how to properly use your utensils. Once you're completely familiar with the proper protocol, go home and set a similar table.

Eating on Location

Hollywood stars do it all the time. They ask if the soup du jour is broth or cream based. They want to know if the dressing can be served on the side. They ask that no butter be used in the preparation of the vegetables.

I do it too. When I did not see anything that was health-conscious on the menu of a restaurant near Bordeaux, France, I was saucy enough to ask a renowned French chef to create a fruit salad for me. It was more delicious than any lapin (rabbit), canard (duck), or escargot (snail), even though it was not on the menu. On another occasion I requested broccoli at a restaurant in San Luis Obispo, California. The waitress kindly suggested steaming stems from the salad bar. I would have never thought of it. When it comes to putting in your order never be shy about politely asking for what you want and what you need.

★ If you simply must have a particular type of sugar or salad dressing, bring your own. A friend who splits his time between Toronto and Palm Beach always carries a special sweetener with him for his travels. The legendary Carol Channing has been known to pack her special brand of salad dressing in her purse.

★ Most of us do not look so wonderful while we are eating. That is why some well-known figures have been known to forbid any photos of them while eating. If you want tips on how to look better chowing down, look for any food scenes featuring actress Joan Collins.

★ When you are traveling ask around for restaurant recommendations. Exercise mates, car rental agents, and airplane seatmates have directed me to full helpings of good eating spots. It was extremely touching that, in the middle of covering the tragic bombing in Oklahoma City, locals working at the Medallion hotel, which housed most of the media, offered a list of favored establishments to visiting journalists.

★ Do more than feast your eyes during your next visit to a museum. They often serve up tasty bargains in an artful setting. It's especially true of museum restaurants in France. One of my favorites is the formal dining room at the Musée d'Orsay. There are also more casual offerings. During a recent visit to Paris I could not get my mother out of the food court at the Louvre. She especially likes the fact that the restaurants are reasonably priced, and English-friendly. That meant she did not have to ask her daughter to translate.

★ For at least one time in your life, stretch your role a bit by going to a restaurant *alone*. I was just out of high school when I remember seeing a woman eating by herself in the dining room of the 680 Hotel in Nairobi, Kenya. In the middle of her table was a rose. Perhaps it is a manifestation of my action-adventure leanings but I thought that she looked so glamorous it prompted me to begin dreaming of my own solo flights. But before you sit down for a meal on your own, query friends and acquaintances for places that are hospitable to women dining solo. For the record, Fouquet's restaurant in Paris is not. During a visit during October 1999 it would not let me enter the dining room where I was to meet a friend. The reason was because I was a woman on her own. As I left I saw my unsuspecting male friend seated comfortably inside.

Catering to Your Health

★ Make health handy. One of the most delightful things about going to a spa is that all things healthy are within easy reach. It makes nutritious eating effortless. Infuse that into your home set. Have water everywhere. Cut a bowl full of lemon slices to accompany everything from fish to water. Set up a silver bowl with fruit. Fill another beautiful container with carrots.

★ Make your heirloom recipes sparkle with health. Is it possible to cut down on the fat or sugar without reducing the taste? I revised one of my mother's vegetarian recipes for cottage cheese patties starting with using nonfat cottage cheese. I use egg whites only. Instead of butter I mix in one of those fat substitutes that come in a tub. No one can tell the difference.

★ When you are eating, especially a grand meal, enlist your wardrobe to make you eat better. Wear that skin-tight skirt. It will put the brakes on how much you eat. You'll be less inclined to have a second helping of that flaky hot apple pie if you are wearing Lycra versus that shapeless tent dress.

★ Since we are talking about food in this chapter I want to say something about anorexia and bulimia. It is hard to sparkle from the inside out if you are not filling yourself with foods that make you shine. You can find many painful examples of this by looking at photos of Hollywood stars with eating disorders. You may not be destined to be a size four. A size twelve may be more your star size.

Liquid

★ Cognac is served up in shimmering crystal. Champagne is kept on ice in silver coolers. You sip martinis from elegantly designed glasses. Bring the same glamour to drinking water. Why can't you keep your mineral water on ice in that silver cooler? Plus after you've indulged you don't have to worry about a hangover.

★ Spas routinely add flavor to water by adding a slice of lemon. An informative waiter at a Las Vegas restaurant told me that to emphasize the lemon flavor, place the slice in the glass before, rather than after you pour in the water. Guyana means "land of many waters." And if you were to go to the South

American country you might find some of that water served with sliced cucumbers. Or if you want to add even more color to your water do what spas do and toss some grapes or berries into an ice cube tray.

★ Not getting enough water with your meal? Just ask the waiter to leave a decanter at your table.

I can see you now. You're lounging like a contemporary Cleopatra on your chaise, which compliments your skin tones of course. In the background soothing music is playing. All the while you are munching on exquisite yet healthy finger food served from a silver platter.

Relaxed? Actually you've only just begun.

The stars are God's dreams,
though remembered in the silence of the night.
— HENRY DAVID THOREAU

★

CHAPTER TEN

On Hiatus

Increase Your Sparkle by "Taking Five"

W hen God was creating the world even he took a break after
six days. Having a day of rest is important enough that it
made it into the top Ten Commandments. I get a sense of how
beneficial time out can be every time my computer goes haywire.
Then it's time to turn it off for a while. Give it a rest. More likely
than not when I reboot it will be refreshed and ready to go again.

When Hollywood stars take time off, whether they are between seasons or projects, they call it going on hiatus. It could
mean anything from an exotic vacation to a cozy stay at home.
Whatever you do or however long you do it, scheduling regular
breaks into your life script will add to your shine.

Actress Greta Garbo wrote routine getaways into hers. During her weekends she would instruct her chauffeur to head either north or south of her Los Angeles home. The Swedish star said that whenever she spied the perfect spot near the Pacific Ocean, she would ask her driver to stop. Off she would go carrying a basket of fruit. This vanishing act could last as long as two days. The chauffeur would sleep in the car while Garbo would spend the night alone at the nearest hotel.

The late Linda McCartney followed a similar path. When she and her husband, Paul, would go through tough times she would encourage him to take a drive and get lost on purpose. It was a way of making the former Beatles's troubles seem far away.

Maybe you feel that your life does not compare to a famous musician or a Hollywood star's, but stress for the working Jane and Joe is noteworthy. Job stress costs companies as much as $200 billion a year. *Fortune* magazine reports it's even worse if you're a big shot. Managers who do not take vacations are 75 percent more likely to have a heart attack. So you could say that you are just trying to save your company money when you take your time off. You could also say that you are improving the quality of your life.

If you are still having a hard time believing that you deserve to make a detour in the rat race, you may be surprised to know that even rodents are capable of having a good time. When researchers at Bowling Green University in Ohio began tickling rats they found that they actually laughed. One researcher said the lab sounded like a playground. I hope those rats are not happier than you are.

Put It in Your Schedule

 Do not leave your time off to chance. Make appointments in your calendar to stop and smell the roses.

 Take care of business and go on hiatus, too. Instead of arriving for a 7:30 appointment at 7:29, plan to get there forty-five

minutes ahead of time. Use the time for a leisurely explo-
ration of the neighborhood.

★ Schedule time to be totally out of reach: no fax, no pager, no
cellular telephone. Remember that voice mail will record
your messages, material coming over the fax won't disappear,
and your e-mail messages will be there when you come back
from your break.

★ Shop and stop. I have always been a power shopper but really
slowed down when spending time with some European
friends. For them it is mandatory to stop every so often to sip
some chocolate chaud or mineral water with a slice of time,
followed by a bit more shopping, then sometimes perhaps a
pastry treat.

★ You may already have a bulletin board to keep track of all
your activities. Create a separate one that focuses on leisure
activities for you and your family. Let everyone contribute
suggestions including related photos, newspapers, and magazine articles.

The Five-Minute Hiatus

★ Even if you don't have time to take a nap, just resting quietly
for a few minutes with the lights dimmed and ears plugged
can be refreshing. Statesman Winston Churchill and President Lyndon B. Johnson are famous nappers who also took
care of business. I've done it myself during all-night editing
sessions. It means slipping off to a restroom with low traffic
or using an abandoned office where you can pull up a blanket
and grab forty winks.

★ It's customary for many a Hollywood star to get a massage before a big appearance. In your case the studio may not be paying, but buy your own session at least once. Pay attention to the techniques of your masseuse, then when you have a few extra minutes, stopped in traffic, standing in line, or during a break at the office, do it yourself, to yourself. Rub your feet. Rub your forehead. Rub the palms of your hands. Another option is to pick up a video or book on massage.

★ Schedule time every day, even if it's just five minutes, to do absolutely nothing. We all have at least that much to spare. Make a conscious effort to clear your mind and think about nothing but the wonderful view in your mind. If it is a fragrant path, breathe deeply. If you find things to touch nearby, by all means be tactile. Or get lost in the sound of singing seagulls or cresting waves.

★ After you've done the virtual thing, get real. Take a quick walk. Go to the most beautiful area of your city, your pace no faster than a meander.

★ Make any time you wait in line at the grocery store a mini-hiatus. Instead of getting mad about the man with an overloaded basket in front of you, take the time to browse through magazines you are interested in but never take home.

★ You may have been told as a kid not to daydream. But forget that lesson. Anytime you are seated near a window, look out. Let your eyes dance on a cloud or wonder about the blueness of the sky. Or do what I did recently during a kickboxing class. I stopped and was overcome by the wonder of a hummingbird flitting from flower to flower. Mere seconds into my hiatus I felt brighter.

★ Curl up with a bunch of catalogues filled with fantasy items that aren't particularly practical. But for the sake of getting away, have fun examining them. Make sure all of your credit cards are locked up so you won't be tempted.

★ Take your time when you're washing your hair. It can be very relaxing when you are not rushing, especially if you select a fragrant shampoo and conditioner.

★ Oscar-nominated director Bernard Jafra tells me when he wants to relax, he checks out the stars in the sky instead of watching Hollywood stars on the big screen.

The Spiritual Hiatus

★ Singer-actress Dolly Parton says that on all of her properties she has a chapel where she can talk and "more importantly listen to God." She says she imagines herself "surrounded by radiant light" and dancing with angels. Even if you cannot build a separate chapel, set up an area in your home where you can have your own conversations with God. Decorate this space with peace. Appropriate items would be candles, flowers, and a Bible or other religious texts you treasure. Design it so you can get great pleasure just from looking, touching, or feeling the objects that you gather in this place.

★ "Presidents have only two moments of personal seclusion—prayer and fishing," said President Herbert Hoover. You don't need a fishing pole or stinky bait or even a special room to pray. As you pray don't always ask for things for yourself. It's soothing to send out prayers of gratitude. Or direct a prayer to someone else who is going through bad times.

★ When you need a moment of silence see if you can slip into an actual place of worship. For extra peace and quiet see if the doors are open during off-hours. It doesn't matter if the church is of another denomination. I've had quiet moments everywhere from Paris's Notre Dame to Milan's Il Duomo.

★ Dozens of airports around the world have chapels where you can meditate between flights. Ask your travel agent about the airports you are flying through.

The Solitary Hiatus

★ Spend some of your downtime alone. Use it to do absolutely nothing or to reflect on where you are in your life script. Stop and listen to yourself and you might discover that you need to do some fine-tuning. Or perhaps a total rewrite.

★ Your greatest ideas sprout while you are alone. They will sneak up on you in these moments of solitude when you least expect it. So keep a pen and paper handy to record your bon mot.

★ Use that time alone to play out your next scenes in your head. Soar. When you are alone you don't have to explain or defend your dreams to anyone.

★ Turn your life into a silent movie. There are hundreds of silent retreats around the country where civilians can go. Or figure out if there is a way that you can bring the sounds of silence to your home.

The Altruistic Hiatus

★ Doing for others is a great way of getting away from your stress. And you do not have to be a part of an organization to help. When you know someone in your church needs child-care while she goes off for job interviews, play baby-sitter. Offer to get your elderly neighbor groceries. Make up gift baskets and take them to the nearest shelter. My volunteer turn began as a child when my mother got me knitting band-ages for an African leper colony.

★ Mix volunteerism and your vacation by signing up to do good works during your time off. Help build a school. Support conservation. Save a whale.

The Creative Hiatus

I can paint for hours and lose track of the world around me. And that's whether I am painting pieces of furniture or a portrait. When I'm finished there is something for me to have and hold that is tangible, unlike when I create material to be broadcast on television. In spite of her hectic schedule, TV personality Katie Couric frequently talks about her love for découpage and how it helps her relax.

Experts describe such activities as a form of "active" medita-tion. There's got to be something to this craft thing, or why would mental hospitals encourage their patients to get involved in activi-ties such as basketmaking? If crafts provide therapy for someone who is severely disturbed, imagine what they can do for you.

★ Perhaps you've been so wrapped up in working and taking care of your family that you've forgotten what makes you happy. Make time to audition pursuits for your time off. Begin by collecting school catalogues and start circling courses of interest. Then take the class that makes you glow the most.

★ If you're still having trouble deciding between classes on knitting your own fishnets and learning to play the kazoo, look to your surroundings to guide you. Around me I saw a collection of hats that included a red Kangol beret and a black feathered number that prompted me to take a hat-making course.

★ Arts and crafts can make your wait time productive. Some actresses knit or needlepoint while they are waiting for their scenes in their trailers. Actress Neve Campbell handles some of her downtime creatively by making jewelry in her trailer.

★ In the movie *How Stella Got Her Groove Back* Stella's much younger boyfriend does a makeover on a dusty, musty room that she once used to make furniture. Winston wants to encourage his lady to continue with her interest. Is there a place you can make a bit spiffier so you can return to a long-lost love of crafts? Are you wasting a room vacated by a child who has left the nest? Can you say Neo–Norma Desmond? Why not enlist that room for your hobbies?

The On-Location Hiatus ·

Singer-songwriter Joni Mitchell writes about being "unfettered and alive" while in Paris. Musician Jimmy Buffet sings that changes in latitude bring about changes in attitude. No question that your location affects your sense of well-being.

When Alanis Morissette became overwhelmed by the success

of her album *Jagged Little Pill* she had to flee her normal haunts. She went on to find peace and anonymity in India and later she went to Cuba. It was while she was chilling in Cuba that she found inspiration to take up music again. Taking that break from her normal surroundings made it possible for her to be reenergized. Getting away can do the same for you.

Okay, so you can't necessarily afford to go to India or Cuba. There are still other ways to, as singer Stevie Wonder put it, treat yourself to all the pretty places in your head, with or without a passport. Going on location can mean going anywhere, far and near.

★ Turn that blasted commute to work into a blessing. Listen to a book on tape that you've never had time to enjoy. Play show tunes that your family won't let you listen to at home. Play that license plate game you loved as a child.

★ Many cities in Europe have a "vieux" section, the old part of the ville where you can surround yourself with architecture from another age. Is there such a place in your city where you can wander through?

★ My home has become such a peaceful place that when I am out and want to go on a mini-hiatus, I go into home furnishing stores. I feel instantly relaxed thinking of home. During these excursions I just browse, no buying. Do you really enjoy the art of correspondence? Go into a stationery shop. Looking for some laughs? Take a mini-tour of a T-shirt shop and check out the humorous sayings.

★ When appropriate appreciate the scenery along the way of your destination. It's something video photographer George Adams does. We were on assignment driving around Idaho back country. I felt pressed about putting together my segment. He, on the other hand, had the right idea by stopping

the car for just a few moments to take in our spectacular surroundings.

★ There is something about just *being* in a spa that is relaxing.
There are more and more options these days including
budget spas and day spas. Find out what is available near
you in your price range.

★ If that's out of the question find a friend or relative who will
let you spend a few hours or days at her home. Return the
favor and make your home a haven for a pal. Go heavy on
the candles and bubble bath.

★ Maybe you don't have two weeks to go somewhere. Take
time where you can find it. One study found that 97 percent
of the vacations taken by Americans were over long weekends. Keep your eye on the calendar for days you can slip
away.

★ Take a sketchpad with you on your next trip and draw your
favorite sights. You could be in Paris or the neighborhood
park. You don't have to be Mary Cassatt or Michelangelo, but
sitting down and studying that church stained glass or flowers on a windowsill will force you to notice things you would
not appreciate otherwise.

The Nostalgic Hiatus

★ Take a hiatus by going to see an animated movie. It will take
you back to your childhood. Make it a real getaway by not
taking the kids. Next time. Take it a step further by zoning
out and watching back-to-back cartoons on Sunday morning.

★ For a nostalgic break, play the games of your youth: jacks, hopscotch, jump rope. It will be a flashback to a simpler time in your life.

★ Remember as a child you could make games from something as simple as the license plates you saw on your family vacation. Use your mind to take similar flights of fancy whenever you have a spare moment.

★ Read aloud from a children's book or your favorite comic book. Perhaps you may have a vintage one in storage somewhere. If not, look in the bargain pile at your neighborhood bookstore.

★ Get a coloring book. WNBA star Lisa Leslie travels with one along with a box filled with ninety-six crayons. You might have seen her coloring on an airplane. For her the bigger the pictures, the better.

The Sporty Hiatus

★ Sports can be a form of relaxation but just make sure that you are playing for enjoyment rather than playing to win. Too much competition will take away from the fun. Look for costars and supporting players with a similar view and perhaps a comparable level of skill.

★ Do not spend a fortune on equipment for your hiatus activity until you have determined that you really like it. I don't want you to get stressed figuring out how you will pay for new toys. So in the meantime borrow, beg, rent, or take a series of classes before you commit large sums to your leisure activity.

The At Home Hiatus

★ Actress Greta Garbo relaxed in her garden. She said flowers captured her heart more than people or animals. In the presence of petals the Swedish star said she could freely speak of her troubles. Whether you talk to them, smell them, or arrange them in a vase, use flowers to enhance your free time.

★ Is there a smell that you naturally associate with relaxation? Suntan oil? Freshly cut grass? Cookies just out of the oven? Find a way to make that smell readily accessible by getting similar scents at the fragrance counter. Spray it on your bed sheets. Spray it on your wrists. Spray it in your entryway.

★ Collect a library of books capable of taking you away from your surroundings. Photo books are especially escapist because you don't even have to read. Find books of the favorite places you've been or of the places you've always dreamed of going.

The Working Hiatus

★ Don't just put on a happy face at work; surround your office with them. Feature photos of smiling faces only. Keep the moody, pensive poses at home.

★ While you are at it decorate your workspace with other uplifting items. Think: vacation postcards, artwork with humorous sayings, or clips featuring your favorite cartoon character.

★ Designate one piece of serene artwork to gaze at when you need to get away: the ocean, a sunrise, a flower. Give these props star quality by framing them. Thumbtacks are, well, tacky.

The Lunch Break

During my first trip to Europe I was surprised to find that most stores would shut down every day at lunchtime. The owners of these establishments believed that taking a break was more important than making a buck. Back in the United States there was a time that some of the shops on Rodeo Drive, especially those with European connections, would also close midday. Although I don't see any "Closed for Lunch" signs in Beverly Hills these days, that's no reason for you not to take a true lunch break whenever possible.

★ Avoid eating lunch at your desk. Go outside. The fresh air is likely to do you good, even if you can go no farther than around the block.

★ For variety take your peanut-butter sandwich to a museum and eat in the sculpture gardens. Or visit the city gardens. Explore something new.

★ When you are making that lunch, select ingredients and packaging that are totally joyful: playful containers, colorful wrapping, unusual garnishes.

★ On some days make your meal the supporting player, your break the star. Instead of eating a long lunch schedule a massage. Do some stretches. Get your nails done.

I hope you are already feeling more relaxed. Being cool and calm will imbue you with the kind of shine that this book is all about, the kind that comes from the inside out. Writing in scenes of peace and quiet into your life script puts you in the perfect position to stay the course. Especially when you are faced with inevitable plot twists.

Through struggle to the stars.
—RAF Motto

★

CHAPTER ELEVEN

Crisis Points

Deal Positively with Negative Plot Twists

I'd just come back from a morning walk on the sunny streets of Los Angeles when my beeper rang out. A storm was about to arrive. There had been all kinds of rumors about the future of *America's Most Wanted*. The morning paper seemed to confirm one of them. In listing the schedule for the next season, *USA Today* reported that the hour show was going to be cut back to half an hour. I was in the middle of an assignment for the show and began wondering how the change would impact me. Then I was paged.

"The show's been cancelled," reported one of my supervisors, who wanted to make sure I got the news, even though I was thousands of miles away from the show's Washington, D.C., headquarters.

Minutes later, I got more stunning news. Burke Stone, one of the most passionate reporters on the program, had just died. I still hadn't recovered from when I had seen him in the hospital just a few weeks earlier. He didn't even recognize me then. His brilliant mind had been short-circuited by the AIDS virus. I was devastated. Immediately Burke's death put everything into perspective. I had lost a dear friend. Losing a show did not seem so important.

In coming weeks the apparent cancellation also made me see who really cared about me. There were people who wouldn't take my calls. Others wanted to make sure they immediately collected on debts. Then there was my mom who sent me food in the mail. For sentimental reasons, some of her dried soup packages are in my cupboard to this day. In the end the show was "uncancelled." But it's a plot twist that I am grateful for because of what I learned.

In the movies, crisis points define the protagonist. The more our hero or heroine endures, the more we cheer. We wanted to see Rocky Balboa lose a few bouts before winning the big fight. In real life we love hearing stories about Sally Jessy Raphaël getting fired eighteen times before going on to become television's longest reigning talk show host. Even television host Regis Philbin has found himself out of work a few times, including one stretch of unemployment that lasted a year. That came long before he ever asked the question "Who Wants to Be a Millionaire?"

Then there is the tale of actor Dustin Hoffman who ended up on unemployment after his success in *The Graduate*. To further his shame *Life* magazine got a picture of him lining up for his check. Dustin says his embarrassment prompted him to push for a part in another movie you may have heard of: the Oscar-winning *Midnight Cowboy*.

You probably did not know that the first album of the singing star Jewel sold at a modest rate of fewer than 500 a week. The cool reception to her efforts forced her to stay on the road doing one-night stands at clubs around the country. She faced boos and rejection. But she also polished her act. Those live performances led to album number two, *Pieces of You*. That earned her a top-ten slot on the record charts.

Darlene Love was a popular singer in the sixties, but by the eighties she says she was cleaning other people's houses. Then she had an epiphany while scrubbing a bathroom commode. At that moment the singer heard one of her songs on the radio. Darlene decided it was time to change her life and she began calling around for work. If you have seen any of the *Lethal Weapon* movies you have seen Darlene. She stars as Danny Glover's wife. You glow girl. All of the above used twisted plots to their advantage. In the end their crisis points were turning points that refined and defined them.

Review Past Performances

You may not have done a very good job of dealing with a similar crisis point in the past. That was then. Don't be a Neo–Norma Desmond. You have another chance. This time you can shine through. Be analytical and think about how you might be able to avoid a rerun. Perhaps by acquiring an in-demand skill, casting a cadre of strong supporting players, or developing a healthy bank account to rest upon.

★ Spend time researching the crisis points of real and imaginary characters. Go to the library. Buy books. Study the critical scenes. Examine how these characters successfully resolved their problems. How can you apply that to your life?

★ Is there a movie out there that deals with your particular crisis point with a sense of humor? For example, do you have a churlish boss? Rent *9 to 5*. The stars of the movie figured out ways, outrageous though they were, to make their work environment more positive. Going through a difficult divorce?

Check out *The War of the Roses.* As you laugh through this very dark comedy it will make you appreciate how devastating the wages of bitterness and hostility can be.

★ Because of satellite technology the world mourns collectively no matter where tragedy strikes. We suffer together, whether the event takes places in Oklahoma City or Okinawa. So when you think you have the worst of it watch the news. It may help you realize that's not true.

★ Don't let crisis points loom bigger than they truly are. Author Richard (*Don't Sweat the Small Stuff*) Carlson wrote the book on separating what is really a crisis point and what's a blip on the radar screen. His conclusion is that it's *all* small stuff.

★ If you think you are dealing with the "big stuff" then spend an evening reading the chapter of Job. He endured so much it may provide inspiration.

★ In Malawian culture it is customary to regularly consult elders for their wisdom. A crisis is an opportune time for you to talk with the seniors in your circle. They have, in fact, been there and done that. They lived to tell about it and share their solutions with you.

Get It Out

In the movies fake tears are generated in a variety of ways, including with the help of secret liquid vials secreted in an actor's hand. If you are not feeling so good, have a good cry—a real one. Researchers have found that there is a difference in the composition of tears that come from an eye irritation versus tears prompted by sadness. This leads scientists to believe that crying may help get rid of substances that are built up in your body because of emotional duress. But keep the tears to yourself, unless you are with the closest of costars. I know it sounds as though I am promoting stoicism but I think that you can become very disappointed when they don't give you expected sympathy. See if you can dash off to the nearest bathroom and let it flow.

Costars, Supporting Players, Fans, and Villains

★ If you need help outside of yourself in dealing with your crisis point, go for it. There is no shame in doing so. Share your burden with your family or professional listeners.

★ See if castmates will accompany you on location if you face a crisis point away from home. Take a friend with you to court, to the hospital, or to the police station. When Oprah Winfrey was going through her legal beef in Texas, her supporters accompanied her to court. It was a rough ride that she planned for, right down to her supporting cast.

★ As contagious as moods can be, now more than ever surround yourself with upbeat, optimistic cast members.

★ If villains have a role in creating your crisis point think of talk show host Christina Saralegui who says, "When I am attacked, I know I am winning."

Dialogue

★ When actress Delta Burke was not faring so well on the set of the television show *Designing Women* she found a way to muster strength to face audiences. Before taking the stage she would look in the mirror and say to herself, "I am a star." Delta says she could see the transformation right before her eyes. Feed yourself the same line when you need a boost.

★ Whenever you feel your life is falling apart, take a page from Eddie Murphy's character in the comedy *Bowfinger*. He kept repeating to himself, "Keep it together, keep it together." On more than one occasion it has helped me keep it together.

Improvise

Movie and television producer Lynda Obst says that in spite of the best pre-production there are often times that things do not turn out as planned. Sometimes Lynda says the director will try to force things to meet with original expectations. But she says it's the brilliant director who will see that the unforeseen is often for the better. Appreciate the unexpected.

As you play your starring role there is always that chance that you will stumble on your way or forget your lines. Improvise. Look at the materials you have and think about ways to reshape them to suit your purposes. What did Scarlett O'Hara do when she lost it all? She gritted her teeth and went forward, making a fashion statement out of draperies.

Editing

★ If you see unhealthy patterns emerging when it comes to your crisis points, cut it out. Why are you constantly feeling sick? Is it because you are not taking care of yourself? Why are you struggling every month with your bills? Are you simply using your credit cards too freely? Enough already.

★ Don't concentrate on all of the bad things that "might" happen. Concentrate on the good that has happened no matter how meager those moments seem to be.

★ It is the job of Washington spin doctors to put the best twist on any situation. Look for ways to do the same with events in your life. It may seem a bit artificial and even ridiculous at first. But then you might discover that spinning helps a positive attitude go further. For example if you lose your job, a serious situation no doubt, spin the situation so you look at it as an unexpected, unpaid vacation. Doesn't that sound better than calling yourself a no-good loser? Of if you've lost the love of your life, spin it so you tell yourself that you're now available for dates with Prince William. Calling yourself a pitiful spinster is not going to cut it. When I was growing up awkward and homely I thoroughly convinced myself I was a swan-to-be and I went on to spin that into reality.

★ Now more than ever you may be struggling to find anything to be grateful for. That's why it is imperative to sift through everything and come up with at least five things you are thankful for every day.

★ Tune in to the happiest music of your soundtrack. Play it over and over and over again.

Do Something

It may be hard to believe because of his current success, but there was a time when *Today* show cohost, Matt Lauer, was jobless. This came after years of a nomadic career that had him in television jobs around the country. Instead of crying about his state of unemployment, Matt saw an ad for a tree surgeon and he applied. Three hours later he got a call from New York television station WNBC. That would lead to substitute host gigs on the *Today* show. I believe that the fact that he did not wait at home for the phone to ring led to his ultimate success.

When publicist Makeda Smith found herself battling her own crisis points, which included physical abuse, she bunkered down and went to school at USC. Not everyone supported her in her quest for higher education. There were villains on the sidelines who Makeda says were clearly hoping she would fail. Instead she soared. Today she oversees some of the hippest events in Hollywood. I encourage you to go out and make things happen, too, when you find yourself in times of trouble.

★ Start mending things: the dress that needs a new hem, the socks that have holes in them, the blouse that needs new buttons. Fixing things can help repair your soul.

★ Clean the house. Your situation may have made you feel helpless. But with cleaning, when you scrub the sink, it shines. You can't help but have a sense of accomplishment.

★ Write on. Putting your crisis points down on a piece of paper is actually good for your health. A study by the American Medical Association found that committing your rough times to pen and paper reduces symptoms of chronic illness. Asthma and rheumatoid arthritis patients who wrote about their troubles for twenty minutes over three consecutive days had significant reductions in symptoms when compared to folks who just wrote about their daily plans.

Keep Looking the Part

You'll have your hands full just trying to make it through your crisis points, but please make time to take care of yourself. Looking bad won't be helpful unless you are going out for the role of martyr. You may think that your new look will help generate sympathy. But doing so simply stalls your opportunity to rise and shine.

The day Princess Diana's divorce became official she did not hole up in some musty castle. Instead, she went out to a charitable event where she looked positively dazzling. Do the same on days you feel defeated.

When Ivana Trump broke up with the Donald, she didn't cozy up with a pint of ice cream and a filled cookie jar on her recliner in front of the TV. Instead, she brought in a personal trainer. She got a new hairstyle. Rumor has it she even had a little nip and tuck. If she felt better about herself in the end, why not? If you'll feel better about yourself, why not you, too?

★ Going though a crisis point is an ideal time to reassess your star style. Do an Ivana. Reinvent yourself. Go for a makeover. Ask a friend, a magazine, or a television show for help.

★ Your crisis point may involve special appearances: a meeting with the school principal, a court date, a funeral service. Take time to pull yourself together. It will make you feel better, guaranteed.

★ Make sure you are getting your exercise. Gaining strength physically is sure to help you feel stronger mentally. Besides, growing saddlebags will do nothing to make you feel better.

★ Eat well. It will look good on you. Overdose on sumptuous but nutritious foods. And now is the time to make sure that you bring out your best props—the best china and silver.

False Sparkle

I was shopping at Barneys New York when I thought I recognized a familiar face. The golden blonde was buying hundreds of dollars worth of cosmetics. After a quick glance I could see that her face was ravaged by unhappiness. It was quite a different image from the one she has presented in *Vogue, Vanity Fair,* and other glossy magazines. My observation was interrupted when a clerk came to help me with my purchase. I asked, "Is that ___?" "Yes," she replied. "And she's stoned out of her mind."

How disturbing. This world-famous woman worth millions was high, and it was barely noon. She had the money to afford the best of everything: sparkling gowns, sparkling champagne, sparkling diamonds, but there was no sparkle in her eyes. She struggled to negotiate the steps out of the cosmetics department. As wealthy and well known as this woman is my first thought was to feel sad for her. It seemed clear that she was dealing with some kind of crisis point. Her antidote was what I call false sparkle: drugs and alcohol.

I call those substances false sparkle because they may seem to make you shine, but they do not endure. They certainly won't help you with your crisis point and they are more likely to produce more. I've seen it happen to people I care about. False sparkle has led to drug debts, diminished interest in life, and even death.

Over the years I have been offered drugs countless times. Including one incident when I was in a recording studio shooting a story with a female rock star. My answer has always been no for a number of reasons, including a rather frivolous one which is I'd rather spend the money on shoes. That way at least I have something to hold on to after the storm has passed.

For a moment, forget about it being right or wrong. The fact is you can't shine when you abuse drugs or alcohol. A urinalysis may be one sure test of drug use, but I've been pretty accurate in detecting drug use when I see the sparkle go out of a person's eyes. Look in the mirror to see if you've allowed drugs or alcohol to rob you of the stars in your eyes.

From hotlines to support groups there are places where you can get help with your addictions. Use them.

Next!

Barry Diller has gone through numerous crisis points during his legendary career as a media mogul. That's one of the reasons I have taken every possible opportunity to talk with him at parties in Washington and Los Angeles. But I was most struck by a story in a book by producer Lynda Obst. In *Hello, He Lied: And Other Truths from the Hollywood Trenches* Lynda says reporters came to Diller for a response after he lost out on a big business deal. He offered no excuses. He blamed no one. His answer was quite simple. "They won. We lost. Next."

A true star doesn't let any grass grow under her setbacks and disappointments. She immediately analyzes why an apparent negative is a positive. This leaves little time for pity parties. While others are wallowing in their reversals a star moves on. The more time you spend wallowing, the less time you have preparing for your stunning comeback.

★ Put a time limit on how long you will wallow. Exercise star Richard Simmons gets out a timer in the shape of a tomato when he is feeling low. He sets it for five minutes. As it ticks, he thinks of his troubles. The timer goes off and Richard says he goes on with his life.

★ Review chapter 10 and look for ways of bringing more pockets of calm into your life.

★ Steel yourself in the knowledge that this scene, this crisis point will be over with at some point. Make a list of the first things you will do when your plot twist has straightened out.

★ *Next!*

I Can See Clearly Now

I did not mean to bookend this chapter with the passing of someone else in my life, but I can't think of a more profound crisis point than the death of a loved one. I write this just having come back with my mother from the funeral services of my beloved uncle, Cameron Akim Msumba, M.D. All my life I was so proud of him. He started his life as a barefoot and orphaned African child and grew up to become a respected cardiologist in Andover, Massachusetts. When I told him that I had received the contract for this book, it was his turn to be proud of me. And no one was prouder. Just before he passed away I was juggling a number of activities on my schedule, including coping with a busy holiday season, trying to entertain a close friend from Europe, surviving a serious case of the flu, preparing to lecture at my university alma mater, doing pre-production work on projects spawned by my own television production company, and finishing this book. All worthy projects but I was feeling crushed by the weight of what I had to accomplish.

Then I got word about my uncle. In the wake of my family's loss everything became transparent. First I had to mourn and honor my uncle and support my mother in her grief. Then it was time to get back to work and focus. Minutes after I arrived home in California from the services I was back at work on the computer. Losing my uncle gave me clarity about my plan and purpose. It also gave me a sense of urgency and reinforced my feelings that what I am doing in my full life is right.

As you work through your crisis points do everything so the experience makes you better, not bitter. Now is when a strong motivation will ground you. Refer to it. If you know that your life script is for the good, trust in your faith and your God to pull you through.

And know that I am a supporting player as close as these pages in your hands wishing you the best. Believe me, I know in spite of my blessings that life is a minefield of crisis points. But when you dwell in your sorrow you can't go forward. Only by moving on will you be able to embrace your happy endings. Plan on having many of them.

> He turns not back who is bound to a star.
> — LEONARDO DA VINCI

★

CHAPTER TWELVE

Happy Endings

Direct a Glittering Outcome, No Matter What

Johnny Carson could see that network executives at NBC television were looking to make some changes. But before they had a chance to nibble away at his successful talk show, he walked away, leaving his dignity, mystique, and popularity intact. He did not give us a chance to get tired of him.

Michael Jordan was still flying through the air when he quit playing basketball. He had already followed his heart to the baseball field and back to the basketball court before finally deciding to leave his days as a player behind.

In spite of many incentives—millions of them, to be exact—Jerry Seinfeld decided to walk away from his extraordinarily successful television series. After seeing the hundredth farewell magazine cover, I did get to the point of saying "enough already." But all the accolades were further proof that Jerry had left his audience wanting. He enhanced his star quality because, like the gambler, he knew when to hold 'em and when to fold 'em.

The biggest celebrities have the gift of timing. They know when it's time to make an entrance and they know when it's time to say good-bye. It's a quality that shines through whether you're at a party, premiere, or planning the final scenes of a job move.

If you stop and listen to your heart, you will know when it is time to move on. Actress Greta Garbo was one of the first Hollywood stars to leave a career when she was still at her peak. Her explanation was simple. "I could not portray anyone better than I had in my previous pictures."

I was not so clear-eyed when I made the decision to walk away from my television job in San Diego to go across country to work for the Fox network. At first I turned it down. I grappled with a decision that meant that I would be leaving the costars I loved most. When I finally said yes it literally made me sick to my stomach. Many colleagues thought the decision was a slam-dunk, due to the fact that I would be going from local to national television. That did not draw me to my new role as much as having the opportunity to do longer pieces from locations around the world. Another part of me knew that it was time to move on so I could grow.

My role with Fox put me in contact with a whole new cast of literally thousands of costars, supporting players, fans, and, yes, even villains. Sure there were some rough spots. But so many fantastic scenes in my life would have never played out if I had not taken on that role.

When I worked in local news a well-respected coworker decided to move on. The reporter and the news director didn't always get along. They had butted heads on a particular piece when the reporter did a story in rhyme, a la Charles Osgood. The news director was very public about his dislike of the story. He went as far as posting a critique on the newsroom bulletin board. So as this veteran reporter was leaving, he saw an opportunity to strike back. Understandable. He posted a farewell note, written in rhyme. Sure, it was funny and even clever. But it also made me wonder, why didn't he just let it go? He was moving on to a job he really loved. Why not make his final scene more about his glorious future and the highlights of his past rather than about retribution? As you move on to greener pastures, don't litter your former pasture with manure.

Castmates will not always make your exit scenes easy. *Partridge Family* star Danny Bonaduce says he found out that his show was no more when he arrived at the studio and the gate did not go up. The security guard asked, "Didn't they call you?"

I could tell how hurt Christie Brinkley was when she told me about the way she was was treated by a cable news station. One minute executives were telling her how great she was, and the next minute her show was off the schedule.

A San Diego anchorwoman I will call Donna found out that she was going to be replaced in an especially brutal way. (For the record, she did not work at my station.) She and her male costar had just completed a weekend newscast when a female visitor introduced herself to Donna's male coanchor as his new weekend coanchor. That was the first Donna heard that she was being removed from her position.

As brutal as exit scenes can be, don't forget that although someone else may close the curtain on one part of your life, you and only you are the one who can decide what happens next.

★ Once you have made your decision, don't second-guess it. Self-doubt will siphon your sparkle. Don't keep popping up at your old haunts. You've heard the expression, "How can I miss you if you don't leave?" Don't be like Lot's wife. She's that biblical character who turned to take one more look at Sodom and Gomorrah, even though she had been warned against eyeing the evil empire. She instantly turned into a pillar of salt. Think of her as you move forward with conviction.

★ As you make your exit, don't waste time thinking about everyone who has done you wrong. Instead, make sure to thank everyone who has helped you along the way.

★ Because life is not a movie, once you have achieved Act III it's not the end. We never know when we'll be making that final bow. But you have the opportunity to update and revise your life script every day. Plan a sequel to your blockbuster. Find a new goal. Uncover another path that will give you another opportunity to reach for the stars. Forever search for ways of setting yourself up into new situations where you can shine, doing things you love with people you love. Never stop believing that you will have a happy ending. And you will.

Roll Credits

Credit is a big part of Hollywood. And I'm not talking about American Express cards. I speak of the kind of credits that come at the end of every movie and television program and on billboards and newspaper ads. How an actor, writer, or director is credited can be a major part of contract negotiations. Agents wrestle for their client's name to go above the movie title. There are also fights for whose name will go first and whose name will be the biggest.

Pick up any of the industry trade papers and you'll find them filled with actors, producers, and networks giving themselves credit for appearances on various shows or for getting recognized with various awards. There are whole editions of industry publications devoted to giving credit to what great guys Arnold or Sylvester are. Studios and colleagues pay hundreds of thousands of dollars to place ads paying homage to the star du jour.

When you think about it, the biggest nights in Hollywood are devoted to giving credit: credit for the best performance by a supporting actor, for the best comedy, the best screen kiss. Of course, I am talking about the burgeoning world of awards programs. One account in 1999 found that there were more than 3,000 trophies handed out in 332 Hollywood ceremonies. That's an event for almost every day of the year. While you don't have to get out the klieg lights and red carpet, giving and getting credit is an essential part of your starring role. I am talking about credit that goes beyond getting an Emmy or an Oscar.

Too many of us postpone celebrating our accomplishments. And curiously as much as Hollywood likes to give itself credit professionally, that's not always the case in the personal realm. So you get an agent, but you put off celebrating until you sell a screenplay. You sell a screenplay, but you wait to celebrate until your opus is made into a film. Then you hold off until the movie makes over $100 million. If you wait too long to bask in your accomplishments you may want to consider Gwyneth Paltrow. She appeared overwhelmed and teary-eyed when accepting the Oscar for best actress in 1999. She got the external award but it seems she was not giving credit to herself. The pressure from her staggering success kept her from fully shining at a stellar moment.

You may have done the same thing by postponing your joy about getting an entry-level job at a television station. You don't want to do your celebration dance until you get an anchor spot or an Emmy or a berth at the network. You've seen the stickers: "Don't Postpone Joy." Don't postpone giving credit. Whether you are giving it to yourself or to others.

An award-winning life means that you shine the spotlight on accomplishments, large and small. Start celebrating today. Acknowledging your achievements and the success of those around you encourages you to keep reaching for the stars.

Giving Yourself Credit

★ Shiny gold statues are not the only symbols of success. Awards come in many forms so be creative. Before her long-awaited Emmy, *All My Children* actress Susan Lucci received all kinds of awards from her family that celebrated her roles as a wife and mother. They included homemade posters, poems, flowers, and even chocolate cake.

★ When onetime *New York Daily News* headline writer and managing editor of *Parade* magazine Larry Smith scored publication of a magazine article he told me he took the check of $1,000 and went to the bank. He asked for five- and ten-dollar bills. Larry took his stash home and proceeded to drench himself in a steady downpour of money. Try that when you have a special payday.

★ My Emmy, my Golden Mike, and all my other awards are in residence with my mother. She displays them with great pride. But I have a collection of my own, including an over-size candelabra I bought to commemorate getting through an especially grueling shoot. Then there's a pewter crocodile stapler I bought to pat myself on the back for giving a successful speech. Script consultant Dr. Linda Seger is able to sit on her laurels. Literally. After working on a script with actress Lindsay Wagner she used the money to buy a sofa.

★ Along those lines, don't feel bitter when the boss doesn't acknowledge your hard work or success. Instead buy something for the office that will serve as a reminder of a job you know you've done well. Possible reward items could be a silver-plated pencil holder, or an oak tape dispenser.

★ Awards do not have to be physical. When I graduated from college, my present to myself was ten days in Monte Carlo. It might sound extravagant, but I got a great package deal. I also felt I deserved it. All through school I didn't party. Plus I graduated with honors. I've been back to the Côte d'Azur at least half a dozen times since then. But that graduation trip remains one of the happiest ten days in my life, in part because it was a symbol of my accomplishments.

★ Make a sign. You might think that the billion-dollars-plus box office for *Titanic* would be enough acknowledgment of success for the filmmakers. But every time I would drive into the Fox lot in Beverly Hills during the movie's run there was a congratulatory banner spelling out that week's box-office results. Use your fridge or bulletin board to post notice of the victories of you and your family.

★ There are plenty of ways you can give yourself credit that cost under five bucks. Let's start with craft services. Very often we reward ourselves with food loaded with fat or sugar. But this time savor a chilled china bowl filled with luscious strawberries. I consider them an indulgence, even though they are good for me. Or buy a cluster of grapes. Recline on a chaise. Pretend you are Cleopatra. Have your romantic lead feed you, grape by grape.

★ When you get a laudatory letter, frame it. Hang it in a special place. Glance at it every now and then as a reminder of your kudos. Reuse the frame when you get the next complimentary letter. Keep a file of the letters and refer to them whenever you are feeling a bit down. Oprah has a congratulatory college board where she posts notes from the likes of Bill and Camille Cosby.

★ When friends e-mail you to congratulate you, print every one of their messages and post them in places where you will be sure to see them.

★ Save voice mail that bears messages of jobs well done. When you need a boost of energy, replay them.

Make a Record of It

★ Actress Fran Drescher has an ample collection of photographs featuring her in poses that commemorate her achievements. There's Fran in front of a billboard touting a movie she's in. Fran in front of a billboard touting her series *The Nanny;* Fran posing with a fax with news that her show had been renewed. Get the picture? Take the picture.

★ If you are the one being celebrated why not bring your own camera? That seems to be the trend these days. When Kristine Lilly, the most valuable player of the 1999 World Cup tournament, met with former President Bill Clinton at the White House she shot the celebratory scene with her own camera. Cincinnati shortstop Barry Larkin kept himself busy during the All-Star festivities that same year by taping the athletic moves of fellow players. Even if others are recording the events of a big day add to it with images from your perspective.

★ Make sure that someone videotapes all of your family's celebrations. File them away in a special place. How easily we forget our accomplishments. Whenever someone in the family feels as though he or she is not doing much in life, put that video in the VCR and hit play.

Giving Credit

If you want to get credit, make sure that you are giving it. When your costars shine brighter they spread their radiance to you. Paying attention to what they do well is a sure way to turn on the glow. To ignore it can produce all kinds of darkness.

When Tim Wulfemeyer, my former college professor, worked as a television news writer no one said much about his performance. When he asked the newsroom vets how he was doing, they said, "If people are not yelling at you, you are doing okay." That is the operating philosophy of many a news organization. Often the feeling is that employees are lucky to have their jobs. The lack of feedback made Tim decide to leave the station. On his last day the news director put his arm around him and said, "Tim, you're the best writer we've had here in quite some time." He responded, "I wish you'd said that a couple of months ago. If you had I probably wouldn't be leaving." He went on to teach at Iowa State University, New Mexico University, the University of Hawaii, and San Diego State University where I was his student. "I guess we should all be a bit more generous with praise," he says. "It don't cost nuthin'." 'Nuf said.

★ When you have someone special coming over for a celebration, say the grad or the birthday boy, set aside a special parking spot. That's what they do for the big shots at Hollywood studios.

★ Be really vigilant about giving credit to costars and supporting players when you sense that they are going through difficult times. That's when your words of support can have the greatest impact.

★ Observe what people around you take pride in and give credit accordingly. A successful man may be accustomed to people gushing about his wealth. If he is an avid gardener give him kudos for his way with a rosebush.

★ Find out if there is any kind of award for the outstanding community work your son, husband, or mother is doing.

Local libraries have reference books filled with information on awards and honors. Follow through by filling out the appropriate forms.

★ Whenever you see that a castmate has been the recipient of some public credit, be it employee of the year or a nice mention in a newspaper article, make sure to either write or call or otherwise acknowledge their moment in the spotlight. Don't be a player hater.

Final Credits

The shooting location was a cemetery in Las Vegas. I instructed my photographer to roll tape as the casket bearing the remains of an unknown child was exhumed from a pauper's grave. All I could do was cry. As tragic as this scene was my tears were not for the child, a stranger whose murderer I hoped to help catch. They were for Mr. Leon Leaster Bothell, a beloved friend and surrogate father. I called him *Malume,* an African word that means uncle. This precious member of the family was dying more than 250 miles away in San Diego.

As a teenager he taught me to drive. He guided me on my path later in life as well. Malume had no equal when it came to integrity and steadfastness. A World War II veteran and prize-winning yachtsman, he rarely talked about his accomplishments. Instead, he would focus on my latest adventures, no matter how hare-brained. It was guaranteed that he would smile and support me.

Throughout the production of the story in Las Vegas I kept phoning home to see how he was doing. With each call it was devastatingly clear he was fading. A vicious cancer was winning the battle against one of the best people I have ever known.

From the cemetery, the crew and I moved on to the morgue. It was another morbid location that forced me to focus on dying. More calls went out to San Diego. I repeatedly asked my mother, "Should I come home?" "No," was her constant reply. My response was more tears.

While in Nevada I was working with people I knew, Sergeant Kevin Manning and detectives Brent Becker and Mike Franks from the Las Vegas Metropolitan Police Department. They had called me for help in solving the killing of an unknown child discovered in the desert. We had worked together in the past. One story was about the killing of rapper Tupac Shakur. But they had never seen me so upset before. I had never been so upset before. Detective Franks took me aside and gave me what would turn out to be the best advice on how to deal with my grief. He told me to make sure to let my loved one know exactly what he meant to me. The detective advised me to be very specific about saying what I was thankful for. He regretted not doing the same for his dying father.

Sadly it would be a couple of more days before I got to San Diego. The response continued to be "no" to my suggestion that I return. My mother had not wanted to worry me. I should have gone with my heart. How meaningless it was to pursue stories when someone who had shined so brightly in my life was fading.

By the time we reunited my Malume was flickering. He was proud and independent and did not want to be a burden, but he became too weak to drive. Then he could barely walk. So my mother and I camped out, sleeping on the couch and floor of his home. We would be together for almost every hour of the next seven days. We did not want Malume to go to a nursing home so we acted as his caretakers, giving him his medication and taking him to doctor's offices. I even spent one afternoon singing to him. My favorite song from this a cappella concert was "You Are My Sunshine."

I waited for a time when we could be alone. First I showed him a videotape of a Father's Day brunch we shared just a few weeks before. He beamed. By now he had lost a lot of energy and it was getting harder and harder to communicate. He struggled to speak. "My day," he said with a smile as he watched the television. Then it was my turn to try to pack all of my love and gratitude into the thank-you speech of a lifetime.

I thanked him for being so supportive. Malume always had my back. He didn't even wince when I got into an accident in his borrowed car on my way to interview one of the stars of *General Hospital*. His first question after I told him about the fender bender was "Are you okay?"

He would be the first to call whenever my name appeared in a newspaper or magazine write-up. And inevitably he would be the proudest. But he was also there for the down times. Like the night when he got down on the floor to sit with me at an overflowing airport gate. He comforted me as I cried about having to go off to a job where I knew I was not really wanted. It should have been enough that he gave me a ride to the airport in the first place.

I thanked him that afternoon in July in every way that I could.

When I finished I reached over to hug him as he sat in his rocking chair. I felt mostly bones. This former yachtsman had lost so much weight and strength. Even so he hugged me back with remarkable power.

This speech that meant so much to me expressed only a fraction of my feelings. Over the years I had tried to give him tiny tokens of my appreciation. Included among them were coffee mugs from around the world, a boating hat from Bordeaux, France, and an Hermes tie from Beverly Hills, California. As I sat with my dying Malume all of the gifts seemed pretty meaningless. They could not make him run again. They could not take away the pain. They could not prolong his life.

Four days later he passed away.

In the end all I could give him was credit.

Epilogue

As rich as your starring role is, it is not about perfection. It's also not focused on outshining someone else. If anything, you spread the light. You'll feel it, just as you feel rays of the sun shining through your window.

Deep inside, all of us can feel which forces in our lives bring darkness, bitterness, apathy, hatred. And instinctively we know what brings sparkle, health, love, faith, kindness. Count on radiance to guide your path.

There is that saying "the one with the most toys wins." I believe the one with the most *joys* wins.

All we can take from this world is a compilation, a series of scenes. It is up to all of us to produce an abundance of meaningful moments. Pack as much joy and love as you possibly can into each and every one of them. Edit the rest.

If there is one message I would leave you with, it would be *go toward the light*. I think of all the rolling blankets of yellow sunflowers that brightened enormous fields in southwest France. Every day it was wondrous to see their faces turn, en masse, to follow a star, the sun. We can learn a lot from those flowers.

★ ★ ★ ★ ★ ★ ★ ★ ★ ★ ★ ★ ★ ★ ★ ★

CLOSING SCENE
 CLOSE-UP: PROTAGONIST SMILING TO HERSELF

DISSOLVE TO BLACK

FADE IN: END TITLE FULL SCREEN:

She Lived Happily Ever After

★ ★ ★ ★ ★ ★ ★ ★ ★ ★ ★ ★ ★ ★ ★ ★

Acknowledgments

Best Performance by an Agent . . . Jenny Bent.
You saw a spark and instead of putting it out you fanned it. It was
no coincidence that we first met at Starbucks.

Best Performance by an Editor . . . Cherise Grant.
With every cut you revealed yourself to be exactly what you are.
Brilliant. I couldn't have cast you any better.

Best Performance by a Former Editor . . . Trish Medved.
I know you had to leave to follow your star but I don't think it was
happenstance that you were wearing a starfish when we first met.

Best Performance by a Mother . . . Dr. Alice Princess Msumba
Siwundhla.
Thank you for your guidance, radiance, and love, my first star, my
North Star.

Best Performance by a Scene-Stealing Costar . . . Christian
Göldenboog.

You made me realize how much better the scenes of my life could be if I changed more monologues into dialogues.

Best Performance by Two Brothers . . . Ralph and Lowell Siwundhla.
You've supported me all my life in spite of not always knowing exactly what your quirky action-adventure sister was up to.

Additional production services provided by: Dr. Harold Bloomfield, Dr. Wayne Dyer, Anita Finley, Larry Smith, Tim Wulfemeyer, Hope Shaw, Jim Dark, Gladstone James, Dave Holloway, Charlie Landon, Jo Mayer, Queva Palma, Brenda Smith, Jim Palivades, Makeda Smith, Alia Unis, Ellen Epstein Benkle, Mary Buckles, Matthew Cibellis, and Allyson Edelhertz.

But most of all I'm grateful to my executive producer: God. Thanks for giving me that original green light and for every single day you extend my option.

Feedback Page

How have you managed to sparkle in the midst of spite? How have you been able to maintain your radiance while surrounded by wrath? How have you been able to dazzle during adversity? Tell me the story of how you are starring in your own life. I want to know!

Come and visit at *www.nozizwe.com*.

You can also reach me at: 311 N. Robertson Blvd., #PMB 455, Beverly Hills, CA 90211

I'll also keep you updated on my speaking and seminar schedule.

Keep rising and shining.

Lena Nozizwe

Printed in the United States
By Bookmasters